Praise for *The Available Parent*

"Duffy's advice for parenting adolescents springs from radical optimism, a form of practical spirituality that recommends being open and available to the possibility of change, essentially exchanging fear and the need to control for hope and positive results. Duffy challenges parents to stop micromanaging and judging their kids and instead acknowledge and accept them the way they are, respect their boundaries and abilities, and let them know they have the power to master their own world. Only then can parents be truly available to provide discipline, direction, understanding, and love in an environment that fosters competence and resilience."

—*Publishers Weekly*

"Raising a teenager can be just as much of an emotional rollercoaster as being a teenager, but clinical psychologist, certified life coach and parenting expert Duffy assures parents that it doesn't have to be such a turbulent ride for either party. Blending self-reflective exercises for parents with words of wisdom from teens and parents whom Duffy has counseled throughout his career, the author raises valid points about the benefits of being an available parent and offers valuable insight into the unique psyche of teenagers."

—*Kirkus Reviews*

"This book is written in a clear, no-nonsense style using observations and examples from Dr. Duffy's work with youth and their families. More than anything else, it is obvious that he understands the teenage mind and the psychological and social factors involved in changing children into adults...I highly recommend this book to parents and practitioners alike."

—Psychlinks

"Dr. Duffy provides a clear, straightforward, doable answer for parents: Stay in touch! Research clearly shows that an open, friendly parent-teen relationship is a major factor in protecting kids from harm. The age-old question for parents of teens has always been: 'How do I relate to these new kids of mine—how should I manage them?' *The Available Parent* provides a clear blueprint for a practical and effective response: Manage the problems you have to, but above all else, stay in touch!"

—Dr. Thomas W. Phelan,
author of *1-2-3 Magic* and *Surviving Your Adolescents*

"Dr. John Duffy's fresh new concept of availability in parenting is an idea that meets the moment. With the pace of society constantly accelerating, we need *The Available Parent* now more than ever! Dr. John's writing is smart, approachable and right on the mark. His blend of practical ideas and colorful examples delivers great insights. Most importantly, I am a better parent thanks to this book."

—Eric Langshur, coauthor of *We Carry Each Other*

"Every parent of a child or teen will benefit from keeping this wise book on their nightstand. It's likely they will want it handy to read over and over again."

—Judy Ford, author of *Every Day Love: The Delicate Art of Caring for Each Other* and *Wonderful Ways to Love a Child*

"I couldn't put *The Available Parent* down because I found my inner voice kept saying 'Yeah, that's right!' or 'Oh, dang, I wish I had known that when my girls were teens.' When I finished reading, I called my two daughters, now in their twenties, and asked them if my husband and I were Available Parents. They both reassured me that we were—and still are. John's a brilliant writer with keen intuition into how kids think and how parents can, sometimes unknowingly, sabotage their relationship. John has used his vast experience to provide parents with the inside dope into how kids view their lives, and what they really need from their parents to make the leap into becoming mentally healthy young adults. Best of all, John relays their amazing stories of growth in smooth, witty, and helpful prose. Any parent with a child—no matter what the age—should read and learn from this book."

—Eileen Norris, contributing writer and editor
of the bestselling *You: The Smart Patient*
by Drs. Mehmet Oz and Mike Roizen

"John Duffy has written one of the most eye-opening parenting books around, an inspiring, important tool for all parents. From his expertise and experience working with teens, John gives us the key ingredient for a healthy, successful parent-teen relationship... being *The Available Parent*. What a simple yet profound title, and what a rude awakening for me! John masterfully defines available parenting and helps parents stop the unhealthy dance with their kids. He gives excellent insight, advice and approaches to become the effective parent we desire to be. And throughout the book, he uses real-life excerpts from teens discussing their issues so parents can understand what is really going on in their world. This is a must-read and is essential to building a healthy relationship with your teen."

—Megan Walls, CEC, ACC,
founder of Conscious Connections Coaching

"I recently read a great book about parenting teens and tweens called *The Available Parent* by Dr. John Duffy, and I'd like to share some insights from this book with you. Even if you are not currently parenting a teen or tween, I think you will find these insights helpful because they contain advice on how to improve any important relationship in our lives."

—Living Compass

"What a true gift. This outstanding book truly gives you a blueprint to fully be available to your teen son or daughter. You will marvel at your teen's sense of competence, can-do attitude, and improved self-esteem. Teens and parents are both resilient; with the tools provided in the remarkable book *The Available Parent*, you and your teenager can both enjoy your new and improved relationship."

—Dr. Kate Smart Mursau, coauthor of
Smart Parenting: How to Raise Happy, Can-Do Kids

"Every parent who wants to give it their best shot in working with, and not in opposition to, their teen needs to check in with Dr. John Duffy and apply his Available Parent strategy. As a professional journalist, author, and mom of three teens who writes about parenting, I was so glad to have found Dr. Duffy in time to give me the tools to quickly understand what it means to be an available parent. To my surprise and delight, as I intentionally make myself more available as a mom, my teens are now purposefully reaching out to engage with me! Dr. Duffy is a trusted guide and cool guy. He truly cares and is all about helping parents and their children find the bright light in each other. He helped to open a whole new channel of communication for me with my teens, and allowed me to appreciate their uniqueness and focus on that, instead of the moments that 'challenge.'"

—Mary Beth Sammons, coauthor of the bestselling
Living Life as a Thank You and *The Courage Companion*
as well as author of *Second Acts That Change Lives*

"*The Available Parent* is a valuable and thought-provoking resource that's filled with many precious lessons and gives parents a unique perspective on cultivating a healthy relationship with their kids."

—Psych Central

"The best parents are those that let their children be themselves. *The Available Parent* looks at various styles of parenting and why they are good or bad. Communication and acting as a mentor, for example, are seen as good things, whereas hovering and lecturing are not. Although brief, it gives a thorough going-over of most parenting styles, with notes on how to make the most effective parent.

The idea of parenting is to raise children that become capable adults, but parents are not fully aware of the responsibility that it entails, or get overwhelmed by the responsibility. This book shows parents how to tend to the path between the two extremes, where the responsibility of raising a child is understood, but there is plenty of room for error and even having fun with them. A parent needs to be unafraid of making some mistakes, and this book shows what the more common mistakes to avoid are, as well as excellent tips on how to take advantage of what tools you have. Better yet, it approaches the matter in a friendly, helpful manner. For parents that are worried about the job they are doing, this is an excellent book."

—Jamais Jochim, Portland Book Review

"There's no better audience for a parenting guide than someone with no kids, right? But *The Available Parent* was a fascinating read. Dr. John Duffy has wisely chosen to reintroduce some common sense into parenting theory. Put your tiger mama to bed, turn all your buzzy electronics off, and just be around for your kids. Wow! Who'd a thunk it?

Apparently, not nearly enough parents. Duffy cites case after case from his therapy practice where kids are ignored or scrutinized, sometimes both at once, by parents preoccupied with Blackberry screens, fantasizing about the future or assessing past actions. With very little time spent just being present with each other, the relationship begins to deteriorate. Simply asking kids about their interests and listening non-judgmentally—being available, in other words—is vital to rebuilding that connection."

—Donkeywork

"Have you ever been bewildered by the changes in your child and your sudden lack of effectiveness as a parent? When hugs and family fun have been replaced by silence, slamming doors and an ever-changing array of moods, you need new tools. Top teen expert Dr. John Duffy has encountered all of this and more in his family counseling practice and offers excellent advice, clear strategies and teen-tested solutions in *The Available Parent*. Dr. Duffy can help you shift the dynamic in your relationship with your teen. Imagine what it would be like if healthy conversations replaced angry outbursts or petulant silence. Using the techniques in *The Available Parent*, you can begin to enjoy a healthy, satisfying, new kind of relationship with your teenager—one based on a foundation of radical optimism, rather than fear-based control. At a time when many 'helicopter parents' micromanage and under-appreciate their children, Dr. Duffy's step-by-step guide is an innovative approach to taking care of teens and tweens."

—Hanging Off the Wire

"*The Available Parent* is a refreshing take on parenting. Dr. John Duffy, family counselor, life coach and top teen expert (an honorific all the more remarkable for its near impossibility) proposes proven techniques to negotiate the ever-changing, seismic shifts of puberty and beyond. What is an available parent? One who encourages a kid to feel heard, understood and supported. Not as a friend, but as an effective parent. The author boils it down for us: 'Our goal is to foster an environment that is most likely to provide a sense of competence and resilience.' And by focusing on our own behavior (which looks as crazy to our kids as our kids' behavior looks to us), we can open the lines of communication, establish trust and try to balance fear with love and acceptance. Parental behaviors that don't work make an all-too-familiar list, including lecturing, micromanaging, smothering, coddling, bribing, waiting and snooping. Luckily, the bulk of the book is all about what does work, along with insider tips and exercises to make us truly available."

—BookPage

"This book came to me just at the right moment, as my older daughter hovers on the edge of adolescence. I'm grateful for Dr. Duffy's wisdom, which I know will allow me to enjoy my daughters' teen years rather than just 'make it through' them. I will revisit this book again and again over the coming years—whenever I need a reminder to be present and available to my kids. It has refreshed my sense of gratitude and appreciation for the remarkable young people in my life."

—Kate Hopper, author of *Use Your Words:
A Writing Guide for Mothers* and *Ready for Air:
A Journey through Premature Motherhood*

the
available
parent

the available parent

Expert Advice for Raising
Successful and Resilient Teens and Tweens

BY DR. JOHN DUFFY

FOREWORD BY
DR. THOMAS W. PHELAN

VIVA
EDITIONS

Published in the United States by Viva Editions, an imprint of
Cleis Press Inc., 2246 Sixth Street, Berkeley CA 94710.

Printed in the United States.
Cover design: Scott Idleman/Blink
Text design: Frank Wiedemann
First Edition.
10 9 8 7 6 5 4 3 2 1

Trade paper ISBN: 978-1-936740-82-6
E-book ISBN: 978-1-936740-93-2

Library of Congress Cataloging-in-Publication Data is available.

To my son, George

ACKNOWLEDGEMENTS

This project has been quite a journey, and I have not traveled alone. My deep gratitude goes out to:

Brenda Knight and the editing and marketing teams at Viva Editions, for their tireless work and professionalism in bringing this book to light.

Eileen Norris, my editor, whose guidance and enthusiasm early in this process was an enormous gift.

Fauzia Burke and the team at FSB Associates, for their care and guidance, and for bringing humanity and clarity to the process of publicity.

My agent, Kristina Holmes at Ebeling and Associates, for her faith in and energy for this project.

Dr. Thomas Phelan and Mary Beth Sammons, the most generous and gracious of mentors.

Michael Hainey and Andrew Santella for their guidance, friendship and support.

Father John Cusick for his lifelong inspiration.

My mom for her strength, and my dad for his integrity and his laugh.

All my friends who lent their expertise, support, and stories, especially Eric Langshur, Liz Flock, Ilene and Mark Collins, Mary Lukens, Dave Burdick, Kate Smart Mursau, Susan Raycroft, Marcy Larson, Matt Nalbach, George and Mary Carroll Dougherty, Chad and Tiffany Owen, and Bob and Lori Donahoe.

Marcy and Marty Dunne, and Jaci and Tony Uhrick, for opening their beautiful homes for the cause.

I owe the largest debt of gratitude to my awesome wife, Julie. You walked with me, patiently and supportively, through every step of this process, and you are the ultimate editor, marketer, and champion. I've learned more about availability from you than any other person.

Finally, my deepest gratitude to all of the teens, tweens, and parents who have allowed me into their worlds. There is simply no book here without you.

TABLE OF CONTENTS

INTRODUCTION TO THE SECOND EDITION . . . . **xxi**

FOREWORD . . . .**xxv**

PROLOGUE AND AUTHOR'S NOTE . . . . **xxix**

INTRODUCTION . . . . **xxxiii**
    The Nature of Availability xxxiii
    Radical Optimism. xxxvii
    The Good-Enough Teenager xxxix
    What Do I Know? xl
    Competence and Resilience xlii

PART 1: YOUR TEENAGER'S WILD WORLD 1
    Too Much Data, Too Little Filter 1
    This Isn't Kansas Anymore 3
    The Adolescent Mind 5
    Social *In*-security 7
    Breaking Away 8
    The Nature of Teen Rebellion 11
    Sex 12
    Intimacy: More Than Hooking Up 17
    Body Image: The Locker Room Terror 19
    What about the Gay Issue? 20

PART 2: WHAT NEVER WORKS **23**

Why Lectures Never Work 23

Why Vicarious Living Never Works 29

Why Micromanaging Never Works. 31

Why Snooping Never Works. 36

Why Underestimating Never Works 39

Why Blinders Never Work 43

Why Judging Never Works 49

Why Smothering Never Works 54

Why Coddling Never Works. 56

Why Overindulgence Never Works 57

Why Bribery Never Works 62

Why "Good Cop, Bad Cop" Never Works 64

The Dad Challenge 65

Why Waiting Never Works 67

PART 3: WHAT ALWAYS WORKS. **71**

CHECK YOUR EGO 71

Don't Make It about You ♦ Emotional Role-
Modeling: Forgive Me, Father ♦ Tapping Your
Intuition

GAINING TRACTION. 86

Deposits in the Emotional Bank Account ♦ Simple
Acknowledgment ♦ The Multiple Benefits of
Laughter ♦ The Ozzy Connection: Step Outside
Your Comfort Zone

COMMUNICATION AND CONNECTION .96

Availability versus Unavailability: The Power of
Music ♦ Other Ways to Connect ♦ Making the
Most of Moments ♦ The Friendship Debate ♦
Shifting the Energy ♦ *Re*-connecting

PROTECT TIME 115
Step Away from the iPhone! ✦ u cn txt ur kid, k?

CALM, CLEAR CONSEQUENCES. 121
Disciplinary Action ✦ Punishment, Rewards, and
Consequences ✦ The Behavioral Contract ✦ When
to Say No: Following Your Intuition

SEE THE LIGHT 130
Fondness and Admiration ✦ Finding Those
Corners Where Strengths Dwell ✦ Supporting
Your Teen's Interests ✦ Fostering Self-Mastery ✦
What about the Weird Kid?

BE THE CHANGE 146
Inspiration by Example ✦ When *Not* to Be Avail-
able: Parent as Consultant

WHY AVAILABLE PARENTING *ALWAYS* WORKS. 155

FINAL NOTE: MY HOPE FOR YOU 159

ABOUT THE AUTHOR 161

INTRODUCTION TO SECOND EDITION

I hate my phone.

Don't get me wrong. It's really cool, the newest iPhone, great apps and all. But I work with kids and parents. And I work with them when things are going wrong, often terribly so. Think about all the events that take place in families, the crises, the miscommunications, the dropping grades, that must precipitate a call to me.

So when my phone rings, when it gets that far, it's bad news. Bad news is my currency in trade. And business is booming. Now, over time, I begin to see patterns in the nature of the familial bad news, patterns that fall within the purview of parents, patterns we moms and dads have some agency over. I find that the bad news can be avoided. This is good news.

But first, I am writing this book and spreading the good news. Now, I have found that it is always a dangerous exercise to revisit something I have written in the past. In order to revise *The Available Parent,* I needed to re-read it carefully and thoughtfully. As I worked my way through the book, I found myself anxious that I might run into a concept or sidebar that I disagreed with, or that no longer resonated with me. I feared a dated reference to Myspace, Lance Armstrong, or the certain demise of Notre Dame football.

Of course, the scariest possibility for me would be discovering that the concept of availability itself doesn't hold up the way I had hoped it would. It's been a couple of years. Maybe it's outdated, or it no longer applies. Well, I needn't have been afraid of that. Every element of unavailability, right down to the idea that it is driven primarily by fear, judgment, and ego, still holds firm and true, more so now than ever.

In fact, I have spent the past couple of years since the initial publication of *The Available Parent* speaking about this concept, teaching about this concept, and revolving my work with families around this concept. I have found, with great relief frankly, that I believe in it more now than ever. It is through availability in which we find fulfillment in the parent-child relationship.

So, availability remains the key to parenting, without a doubt. The difference in this edition is actually a matter of emphasis. In attending to my client families, speaking to thousands of parents, and listening to many more teens and tweens, I have learned recently that we have a true crisis of parental availability today. I have learned that availability is not just a handy parenting technique, but a necessary mindset for parents today. Not just parents of teens and tweens, either, but all parents. And we parents are sorely lacking in availability.

The stakes are enormous. People tell me nearly every day that parenting is the most vital part of their lives, their highest priority. Parents hold the well-being of their children within their lens of awareness nearly constantly. And in an ever-changing world, this is certainly a good thing.

But far too often, we parent through our own ego needs.

Far too often, we pass judgment on our kids.

And far, far too often, we parent through fear.

Fear.

Fear is the wily and powerful block wedged firmly between where you sit now, and effective, enjoyable, connected parenting. I am in the unique position every day of sitting with families in need of change. When parents are fearful, they act differently. Empathy, listening, and warmth are all so easily eclipsed by the fearful parent.

And parental fear has legs. Our kids remember. Oh, Mom freaked out on me. She reminded me I can't trust her when it hits the fan.

I hear that a lot, and it's a very tough mindset to shift.

And today, more than ever before, our children need us as they navigate their unsure way through the slippery maze of noise that besieges them at the speed of sound, forcing them to adolescence and beyond well before their shaken bodies are prepared. Through it all, they need guides, trusted guides.

If you parent from a place of fear, or judgment, or ego, your child is alone. Helpless. Guideless. Yes, the stakes are high.

But if you can find the available parent in you, if you can identify and eradicate the fear, judgment, and ego that binds you, you can reclaim your status as a parent. No matter how far-gone the situation may seem.

You hold in your hand your chance. His chance. Hers. Guide your kids forward with love, clarity, hope, and joy.

And maybe I can get back to playing "Words with Friends" on this thing.

FOREWORD

Suddenly, it seems, you are the parent of a teenager. It's a role you have looked forward to for several years with a good deal of concern and apprehension. And sure enough, now that the job is upon you, you realize it is a different world! Your formerly friendly son now seems more sullen, moody, and distant. Over the last few months your daughter has apparently come to believe that her parents are out of touch with reality. Where are these kids coming from?

As one mother put it, "My daughter went to high school her first day as a freshman and never returned. I lost my baby!" Through things like Facebook and texting, teens nowadays seem to spend their entire days "wired" to each other. When they're not connecting with peers, they are surfing the Internet, playing video games, or watching TV. It's as if there is no more room in their lives for parents. Attempts to communicate at the dinner table, such as the notorious "How was your day?" are met with curt responses like "Fine." End of conversation. Another attempt at pulling teeth has failed.

You feel hurt, rejected, angry, and scared. What if my son starts using drugs? What if my daughter starts having sex? What in God's name am I supposed to be doing with This Kid!?

In *The Available Parent*, Dr. John Duffy sticks his neck out and offers a clear answer: As the parent of a teenager your top priority—before anything else—is to stay in touch with your rapidly changing youngster. Staying in touch is the essence of what Dr. Duffy means by availability. Availability is the ability to understand your child's need to pull away. It's the ability to remember your own teenage years and—even though you may feel rejected at times—to treat your retreating child with respect. Availability is the ability to leave your fears and your ego behind and to really listen to what your adolescent has to say, even if it makes you cringe.

Not an easy task by any means, but *The Available Parent* gives a clear road map for carrying the mission out. Dr. Duffy first takes you inside the mind of a teenager, so you can understand where This Kid is coming from. He then explains why some parents' natural inclinations, such as snooping, micromanaging, blinders, and bribery, never work. Next Dr. Duffy describes the notion of parental availability, and he offers specific methods for recreating the connection with your adolescent offspring. For those who are fearful that availability means laissez-faire parenting, there is a chapter on discipline and behavioral contracts.

The goal of Dr. Duffy's book is to help parents of teens understand and define their job. For moms and dads that means, among other things, accepting the fact that their children are supposed to eventually break away, leave home, and become attached to new people. But the goal of *The Available Parent* is also that teens and parents enjoy one another's company as much as possible now while they're still living in the same house.

What in God's name am I supposed to be doing with This Kid? *The Available Parent* gives you the answer.

Thomas W. Phelan, Ph.D.
Author of *1-2-3 Magic: Effective Discipline for Children 2-12*

PROLOGUE

"Screw you, Dad!" the young man boldly said, fire in his eyes.

"Josh, I've told you not talk to me like that. Now we're here to talk to Dr. Duffy about your grades. How are you doing in that math class? Your mother said she e-mailed the teacher. She seems concerned."

"Fine. I'm doing fine."

"Well, your teacher certainly doesn't seem to think so."

Then Josh, mimicking, sarcastically: "Well, your teacher certainly doesn't seem to think so."

Then Dad, to me: "See, Dr. Duffy. This is what I get. I leave work early, take the damn train up here just for him, and this is what I get. Happens all the time with this kid!"

Skilled therapist that I am, I gently excuse Dad from the room to talk to Josh alone, and hope that things cool down with a little separation.

"Screw you." Josh to Dad as he's leaving.

I love my job.

"You were pretty hard on your dad there, don't you think?"

"Man, he wrote me off so long before I ever wrote him off, I swear to God."

He wrote me off so long before I ever wrote him off. Wow. I knew Josh was speaking the truth. When I asked him to be more specific about what he meant, he went off on a rant:

"Well, let's see. He judges everything I do on the fact that he caught me with pot one time. *One time*, like, three months ago. He doesn't joke around with me anymore. Like my last report card, I had all A's and B's except for Modern Euro, but that's the only one he wants to talk about. It sucks, man. It's like he hates me. He used to be the *man!* He used to be chill. Now, I just sneak into the house and avoid him."

This conversation took place years ago, but Josh taught me a lesson that day that has, quite frankly, been nagging at my psyche ever since. I knew he was sincere and in pain, pain which he skillfully masked as anger. He missed his father's loving presence in his life. He missed the fun they used to have together. Before his eyes, within a very short period of time, his father became unavailable. He became closed-minded, judgmental, and angry. He lost Josh, and Josh lost him. Heartbreaking. As much as his father was confused by Josh's behavior, Josh was confused by the changes in his father as well. When did he get so angry? Why is he so serious all the time? What's with the constant third degree? What happened to the fun we used to have?

And so, somewhere along the line, Josh effectively gives up, accepts that things have changed, that for some reason his father is no longer available to him the way he once was. Josh copes by making himself unavailable as well, and as the love and trust between them slowly erodes, the wall between them is slowly erected. With each unavailable interaction, this wall becomes higher and stronger. Soon, this once caring, loving relationship becomes angry, harsh, and distant. Conflict entirely defines and engulfs the relationship. The scene between Josh and his father may seem all too familiar to you in your family. If so, believe me, it does not have to be like this.

Since that revealing session with Josh and his father, I have witnessed similar phenomena in families, over and over and over again. By and large, I've come to realize that it's not our teenagers who are unavailable. We parents often strike first. We strike with judgment, fear, and ego. Far, far too often, we parents are unavailable, and our children simply react in kind.

AUTHOR'S NOTE: In the interest of confidentiality, all identifying information has been changed.

INTRODUCTION

"To witness fully those precious, fleeting years between childhood and adulthood, what a joy! What a privilege!"

THE NATURE OF AVAILABILITY

They look so different, don't they, than they did when they were younger? Many of those soft, gentle, rounded features of childhood have been replaced with angles, edges, muscle, height, and hair. As preteens and teenagers, they seem pointier somehow. The face that for years wore a perpetual smile now carries something heavier in the brow, something more thoughtful or sullen. You fear loneliness or depression has befallen them. And the way they look, that's just a part of it, isn't it? They act differently, more self-conscious, moody, unpredictable, and concerned. Definitely less joyful. And then there's the way they relate to you. What happened there? Your life together to date has been nearly blissful in comparison, filled with fun and laughter, learning and sharing. That sharing part, that really seems missing today. They really don't seem to want to talk with you or share with you at all. They seem distant and avoidant. Their bedroom is a vault, filled with secrets and answers you no longer feel privy to. You find yourself in the paradoxical position of grieving the loss of someone very much alive, someone you hear snoring, talking on the phone, or tromping to the bathroom upstairs. You feel evermore powerless and afraid. All their lives, you have heard and read about the horrors of adolescence, but always felt that your family would somehow get a pass. But here you are. Yet you know, deep in your heart, that it doesn't have to be this way.

You are right.

If any of this resonates with you, you are right. Even if it has been this way for years, even if the same dynamic played out in your relationships with your parents, and their relationships with their parents, you are right. It does not have to be this way. I am writing this book because I have seen families change. I have been fortunate in my work to witness teenagers and parents reconnecting, doing so in healthy ways, ways that set the stage for growth all around. Yes, parenting an adolescent can be difficult at times, but I know that with the right tools, and a dramatically different way of perceiving these years, you can recapture your bearings and find the joy again.

Yet I find that many of us, in fact, carry biases against teenagers on the whole. Every week, I have conversations with parents of teenagers seeking help, and they often explain their predicament with a winking, nodding, "Well, you know, teenagers..." The assumption is usually that, once they cross into teen years, children become by definition oppositional and defiant and difficult, untrustworthy, up to no good, all as a result of their age, something they have literally no control over. I sometimes think we carry harsher negative stereotypes regarding teenagers than any other group out there. And the biases are, on the whole, incorrect. Each of our kids is an individual, with his own backstory and context that informs his unique personality today. But no teenagers, none of them, are bad people. We know this deep down, that even the most negative behavior from our kids is indicative of something other than inherent evil.

Still, I see parents treating their children like strangers. I see parents displaying so little positive regard for their kids. I often wonder whether parents remember that they were once in teenage shoes themselves, coursing through neighborhoods with similarly weary parents and other untrusting adults. Well, we are parents now. We don't have the option to forget so quickly.

Now, I'm not sure why we as a culture feel the need to hold tight to the dread of adolescence. Perhaps we find some comfort in the idea that *everybody* feels this way about teenagers, so it must be true. Maybe it provides us with an excuse when things go wrong—"Well, like the books say, she's crazy. What can *I* do?" Either way, I think a change in point of view, in which we see our teenagers as the extraordinary individuals that they are, will make parenting them far less daunting and far more enjoyable. For everybody.

Conventional wisdom dictates that teenagers are poor communicators, and that they often stop talking with their parents altogether. In my experience, however, I've found that a parent's anxiety about raising a teenager too often gets the better of him, such that he is less *available* to his teenager. I would argue that, more often than not, the teenager then responds to his parent's unwillingness to listen to and communicate with him appropriately and effectively. This was certainly the case with Josh and his father. In fact, teen after teen has expressed this sentiment to me over the years. Parents find themselves judging their teenagers, and wanting them to be somebody different than they are. Parents often admonish themselves for the fact that their children are not interested in school, party too often, or play video games for too many hours. Through the judgment and the emotional baggage they themselves bring to the relationship, parents too often limit their ability to communicate with influence and enjoy the relationship with their child.

Teenagers are left feeling unheard and misunderstood, and parents are left feeling bewildered by the changes in their child and their sudden lack of effectiveness as parents. The parent has become unavailable, the teen responds in kind, and a negative, often destructive cycle of communication begins.

I can imagine some parents reading the above and thinking: What do you mean? I'm *always* available to him. I drive him everywhere, coach his teams, ask him about school. Well, the truth of the matter is, you can physically be right next to someone an awful lot of the time, and still not really be available to them. If you need them to be something they're not, if you are harsh, criticizing, and judging, if your anxiety is center stage, then you are not truly available.

The available parent of a teenager is open to discussion, offering advice and problem solving, but not insisting on it. He allows his child to make some mistakes, setting limits, primarily where health and safety are concerned. He never lectures—he is available but not controlling. The available parent is self-aware, and keeps his own emotions in check when dealing with his teen. He is unconditionally loving and accepting and open to new and different ways of thinking. As such, he is neither cruel nor dismissive, ever. The available parent is fun and funny and can bring levity to the most stressful situation. All of that is to say, there are no conditions to his availability—it is absolute. The available parent fosters an extraordinary child, teenager, and adult.

I think we have a tendency today to overparent, micromanage, and underappreciate our kids. Imagine for a moment shifting the dynamic in your relationship. If you can get there as a parent, you can begin to enjoy a healthy, satisfying, exciting new kind of relationship with your teenager, a relationship with a foundation not of fear, but of radical optimism.

And we can all breathe easier as a 13th birthday approaches.

RADICAL OPTIMISM

I want to share a phone conversation I had with the mother of one of my teenage clients. She delineated for me all of her fears regarding her daughter, a bright, pretty 17-year-old with slipping grades who had begun experimenting with drinking. She told me, quite honestly, that she was afraid her daughter might "fall off the deep end." She envisioned her daughter dropping out of school, becoming a junkie, and living on the street. She feared that her daughter might not survive her teen years at all. But, wait a minute, Mom! A few margaritas and some C's in school, and suddenly we've got her living in a box? No wonder you're so anxious.

The last thing on this mom's mind was *enjoying* her daughter. Through her fear and anxiety, she could not even imagine a successful, thriving daughter. She was just hoping that she, her husband, and her daughter would simply make it through these years drawing breath! What a dangerous concept for parents: just making it through. *Making it through* does not allow for hope, for joy. It is solely a wishing away of time, and too often we fail to recognize how precious a commodity this time, these few years, can be. Until, of course, the time has passed. And then it is too late.

In the end, the mom in the example above told me she was losing hope. In the few weeks that followed, I asked other parents how they felt, and this hopelessness, to my surprise, turns out to be quite the phenomenon. I often hear parents say something like, "Oh, if I can just get him to his eighteenth birthday!"

As you read this book, I encourage you to place your fears aside in favor of hope and optimism for your relationship. Allow for the possibility that you can rediscover your connection with your teenager. Find your power in the relationship. Guide your teen through the sometimes rough waters of adolescence. Fearlessly provide him the wide berth of freedom he needs to feel strong and competent. Learn to be available as a parent, and feel your relationship evolve.

This book is born of my experiences with families over the past several years: families who have sought my professional help, and those I know personally, those in turmoil and those at peace, available and not so available. My most useful discussions, however, have been with the hundreds of adolescents I have had the opportunity to work with and get to know over the past decade or so. The brilliance, maturity, and simplicity of their ideas have provided me with clarity of vision for this project I never could have found without them. The very notion of the available parent is a product of these discussions. These teens and tweens have driven my own sense of radical optimism.

THE GOOD-ENOUGH TEENAGER

> "Love me like you would have if I had
> turned out the way you pictured."
>
> —AMY, 15

The first challenge for you is to acknowledge and accept your children right now, where they are. Too often, we expect our children to be different than they choose to be. We *judge* them, and the clear message they receive, far too often, is "You're not good enough." I work with many a parent who will present a laundry list of changes a teenager needs to make to graduate to the "good-enough" category. If this scenario resonates with you, consider a life with your teenager that is peaceful, where you choose not to judge her, where you support and accept and love her. You need to know that you can decide, right now, before you finish this paragraph, that from here forward, your child will *always* be good enough in your eyes.

"Good enough" is a starting point, not an ending point. In order to have a relationship with your teen, in order to have influence in his life, you need to acknowledge, accept, and challenge him. You need to respect his boundaries and show that you believe in his ability to master his world. Now, your acknowledgment and acceptance may not mean he is jazzed to sit down with you and entertain a serious talk about grades, but you never know. I've seen a number of situations where a teenager will seek out a parent for help when he's struggling. Believe me, this simply does not happen without acceptance and acknowledgment. This much I know for sure.

Once you acknowledge, accept, and challenge, openly and without judgment, you are available. Then you can really begin to parent. Your discipline will have teeth. Your opinion will matter.

Your voice will be in their minds when your children are making tough decisions late at night. If they believe they're not good enough in your eyes, they'll throw in the towel on your relationship as well. But remember, you will have done so first. Don't be that parent. Rejection of your teen will attract heartache and frustration to you, years of joylessness and fear. Start with acceptance, acknowledgment, and understanding, and you've got something. Be truly available, and your relationship can be among the greatest joys of your life.

What Do I Know?

I have noticed an interesting trend in my practice over the course of the past several years. It's been my true privilege to get to know, in a mutually respectful, genuine way, a large, diverse group of adolescents. When teenage clients seem impressed with an insight I share during a session, I often tell them that their world is easier to see through my eyes because I have the "luxury of objectivity." That is, I am not wrapped up in their story emotionally in the intimate way their parents are, or they are themselves. The luxury comes in handy. Because I am not the mother or father, I hear elements of wisdom in their obstinacy, strains of reason in their interest in video games, breaking curfew, smoking pot, or other habits that parents might describe as "troubling" or "unacceptable," and that we clinicians are often quick to label "pathological" or "antisocial." Over the years, these kids have taught me that before we diagnose and medicate, it would serve us quite well to simply listen, really listen.

Despite whatever difficulties bring teenagers to my couch, I actually get to know their best: their most thoughtful, empathic, intelligent and often hilarious best. My wish is that you, as their parents, experience the same hopeful excitement about your teenagers. You've spent their entire lives with them. You've spared no expense to take care of them. You're the ones who have suffered through Barney and Raffi on continuous loops in the car to soothe them. You've worried about them, fed them, clothed them, and nurtured them. Why should you suddenly lose the joy of these relationships simply by virtue of the fact that they've crossed into a new phase of their lives? Adolescence is so fleeting and wild, such an exciting new adventure. Don't you want to be there for it?

Chances are, the tragedy is not what your teenager is doing in his life right now, or not doing. No, the tragedy would be if you missed it.

The truth of the matter is that my attention and positive regard are a small consolation to the teenagers with whom I work. The other day, in a heartbreaking realization, a young man recognized that I was the closest he had to a father figure in his life. He knew that my support was only a pale facsimile of what he truly needed. Your teen, though he may not say so outright, wants *you*—your attention, love, and positive regard.

As my own child charges all too quickly through his teen years, I am constantly mindful of the passage of time. I want to enjoy him, drink him in at each age and every stage. I find him remarkable, wonderful, and miraculous in so many ways. I know we will have our struggles, fights, and disagreements. I know that I will sometimes be anxious as he walks out the front door and into whatever the outside world brings to him. But I am also keenly aware that I want to know him. Through every craggy patch, I want to *know* him.

And I can envision him already as an adult, beyond the teen years. I think, for many of us, our worst fear as parents is that we will break emotionally with our teenagers, and this break will carry into our adult relationships with them. This is indeed a scary thought. We've all witnessed this before. Many of you may recognize this phenomenon in your adult relationships with your own parents. I firmly believe that if you can remain available to your child through his teenage years, you lay a foundation for a healthy, loving relationship with him in the years beyond. As we grow older, I think we all begin to realize how short life is, how short our time together as a family truly is. Why not set an open, loving, available standard?

COMPETENCE AND RESILIENCE

As confounding as parenting a teen can feel day to day, I want you to keep in mind that our job is actually abundantly clear. Our goal is to foster an environment that is most likely to provide a sense of competence and resilience. Competence and resilience. That's it. As long as you remember this goal when you are confronted with decisions about your adolescent, be it about discipline, bullying, school, drugs, or too much TV, your compass will be pointed in a clear direction, and you will feel increasingly comfortable with your decisions and your decision-making ability, as time goes on.

Further, you need to know that you have *all the influence you need* to be a force in your teen's life. Recent research indicates that the vast majority of teens spend at least three times as much time with peers as with parents. Despite this statistic, research also continues to support the idea that parents remain the strongest influence in the lives of their teens *by far*, in both their beliefs and decision making. You remain your teen's primary role model, and you carry more influence than you may believe.

Your availability will be a function of faith that your influence, in combination with her own inner strength and wisdom, will carry your child through any challenge. If your initial reaction to this assertion is something like "I'm not sure she possesses this strength and wisdom you speak of," I hear you. She doesn't show it. She makes stupid decisions. She keeps getting caught. She's unmotivated. And so on. Despite all the mounting evidence, believe me, if your teenager is like *every other teen* I have met over the years, the strength and wisdom are there. Open yourself up, become available, have faith in her, and slowly, perhaps very slowly, you will begin to see the change. Close yourself off to the possibility of it, assume the worst about your teenager, and you are contributing, rather needlessly, to a self-fulfilling, self-defeating prophecy.

Available parenting differs in a critical way from other self-help parenting techniques. Instead of focusing on your *teen's* behavior, over which you typically, and appropriately, exert little or no control, the focus here is on *your* behavior as a parent, over which you possess virtually full control.

You might be thinking, Why do I have to change? She's the one who's creating all the havoc around here, what with her texting and hormones and all! Well, the truth is, you become available because parenting is a priority to you, because you care so very deeply for your child, and for his future. And, perhaps most importantly, you do not want to be afraid—*of* your child or *for* your child. You inherently know that decisions made from a fearful place in you are rarely the best decisions. You'd rather share communication and harmony with your teen than anxiety and conflict. The most impressive by-products of your availability will be the mutual enjoyment of your relationship and the elimination of dread regarding adolescence. This fits better with the way you want to live your life, and you know deep down it will provide a good model for the way your teen chooses to live her life as she matures.

You are not expected, by the way, to be perfect at any of this. Just raise your awareness. Each shift in your energy will create markedly positive results.

TRY THIS MEDITATION EXERCISE

Indulge me for just a few moments in an exercise. Find a time when your teenager is occupied in a more public area of your home, somewhere other than her bedroom. She may be reading, talking on the phone, playing a game, or listening to music. For the purposes of this exercise, as long as she is occupied, it really doesn't matter. Now, find a comfortable seat in another room. First, I would ask you to gently remove from your mind, just for these moments, any feelings of anger, ill will, disappointment, or resentment you harbor toward her. Take a few moments alone to close your eyes and take a few deep, cleansing breaths. For the next several minutes, assume that all is right with the world. You needn't worry about a thing. You can cast all of your concerns, just for now, totally aside. As you inhale, allow your lungs to fill with a sense of well-being and contentment. As you exhale, envision your negative thoughts leaving you. Once you feel calm, open your eyes. Stand up, go into the room where your child is occupied, and take a seat. Continue your deep breathing.

Just watch her discreetly for a few moments as you attend to your breathing. Sit quietly, watch, and listen. With no demand on yourself, take note in your mind of what you see in her, what you hear from her. Look at the shine of her hair. Allow yourself to marvel at the perfection of her hands. Listen to her voice and her laughter, her very breathing. Watch her smile. In what ways does she look like you? Now, look at your child's beautiful eyes. How long has it been since you have seen them in this way? Breathe in the miracle that is your teenager.

When you feel ready, go back to the room where you began this exercise, relaxing and breathing. Have a seat, and take a few more cleansing breaths. Now, think about your teenager. How are you feeling about her now?

In this exercise, I am encouraging you to see your teenager with the same sense of awe and wonder that you had when you first laid eyes on her, when she was a newborn baby. If you participated fully in this exercise, I'll bet it felt pretty good. If you conduct this exercise from time to time, you may find you get into the habit of appreciation and gratitude for the presence of your teenager in your life. She makes things interesting, doesn't she? She is a force. She can be upsetting and frustrating, yes. This in fact is part of her job. At her core, though, underneath it all, she is wonderful and amazing—a miracle, really. And you as a parent are really so fortunate. You have the opportunity to parent this wonderful, challenging person, to affect the future of her life, your life, your family, and perhaps everyone. A large responsibility, yes, but none could equal the rewards.

PART ONE

YOUR TEENAGER'S WILD WORLD

"When I was her age, I knew it all. Now,
I feel like I know nothing! It's like God's
little joke on me."

—MOTHER OF LIZZIE, 16

TOO MUCH DATA, TOO LITTLE FILTER

Consider, for a moment, the life of your teenager today. He is
bombarded with information: Twitter, Facebook, YouTube,
texting, smart phones, and the multisensual assault from the
Internet, movies depicting graphic violence and sex, iPods, iPhones,
iTouches, iPads and everything else "i." Adolescents spend an
average of six to eight hours a day exposed to some form of media.
Information-riddled screens of all sizes abound in today's adolescent world.

The Internet in particular is the Wild West for teenagers.
There's way too much information available, and with no editor
or filter whatsoever, it's a teenage minefield. In our day, we all
know we had to go well out of our way to find that information

about sex, drugs, and rock 'n' roll our parents didn't want us to see. Now your child can simply log on, and he has access to more data than we ever could have imagined as teenagers. Never has it been more clear that we, as parents, have precious little influence over the information our kids can access.

Keep in mind, also, that your teenager probably *loves* all this techie stuff. Dismiss any of it, and you risk losing his respect and attention. Today, in most cases, we parents need to learn from our teenagers about the things that influence their thinking. We need to concede that our teens know more than we do about the flow of information. Of course, this dilemma provides us with an excellent opportunity to talk with our teenagers, tap their expertise, and learn from them. Ask your teen, "How do you guys communicate with each other? What do you think about it? What do you do with all of it?" Keep asking and express *genuine* curiosity. Teenagers like to be experts and teachers—it fosters their sense of competence. And as a significant bonus, somewhere beneath their radar, your relationship with them grows and deepens.

Now, you need to recognize that there is a paradox at play here. It is true that adolescents today are more tuned in than ever. Teens have infinitely more ways of keeping in touch with one another and on top of information, but this somehow leaves them more *isolated* than ever as well. Despite being in constant contact with friends and cohorts through cell phones, text messages, Facebook, Skype, and interactive video games, a surprising percentage of teens continue to describe their lives as "empty" and "boring." When your teen is online, playing a video games, or tapping messages into her phone, she is often *alone*. As available parents, we need to recognize that our teens are bombarded with unfiltered information. And we also need to understand that this overload does not truly fulfill their social needs.

This Isn't Kansas Anymore

The information overload is not, of course, the only source of stress for your tweens and teens. It's a strange new world out there in other ways, too, and you need to be aware. First, you need to know that use of certain drugs among teenagers is at an all-time high. In many teen circles, smoking pot is not at all taboo, and there is a growing contingent who feel that smoking pot is smarter, safer, and more natural than any other drug, including alcohol. Further, many teens experiment with harder drugs. In my office, I hear a lot about cocaine, mushrooms, heroin, and ecstasy. Many more are prescribed psychotropic drugs, including antidepressants, antianxiety medications, mood stabilizers, and, of course, Ritalin and Adderol for symptoms of ADHD. In recent years, many teens are also sharing their meds with friends. They might sell a few Ritalin to a buddy to get through exam week, for instance, or pass around Xanax at a party. This happens a lot, and in today's teen vernacular, selling drugs in small amounts to friends does not typically count as "dealing." Drugs are no longer the bastion of the obvious burnout. This might be the sweet honor roll kid next door.

Along with the glut of information and the accessibility of drugs, social pressure and academic demands on today's teens are high. Sexuality is a part of adolescent lives at younger ages than ever before. There is so much physical, verbal, and virtual bullying. As harsh as bullying is among boys, it appears to be even more severe and damaging between girls.

Academic stress in particular increases year-to-year on teens. The typical high school student today is assigned three to four times the amount of homework as their parents were given a generation ago. College admission standards have skyrocketed, forcing students to excel academically, taking the most challenging course load they can handle, honors, accelerated, and AP classes. Parents are hiring tutors to guide their kids to the highest possible ACT and SAT scores. As these criteria become ever more inflated and bloated, teens are experiencing a tougher time than ever setting themselves apart from the pack. So, they stack extracurricular activities on top of the academics: sports, groups, clubs, plays. Some kids have two, three, even four meetings or practices an evening. And then they can start homework. On that end, sleep can be greatly affected as well. The end result is often a cocktail of enormous stress and fatigue, beyond anything we experienced as kids.

And some kids, of course, check out. They do little homework, hole up in their rooms, text and play games late into the night, faces lit up by tiny screens. These kids are often referred to me and other therapists, the goal typically being to get them on the treadmill, productive and cranking out resumes like the top of the class. But we have to recognize that these kids are stressed as well. They just choose to manage it a different way. Lacking confidence in their competence and reliance, they disengage. But please, do not fool yourself here. Your couch potato is just as stressed as the top one percent of his class. It's a tough time indeed to be a teenager.

This is scary stuff, and they may not tell you, but a lot of adolescents are overwhelmed themselves. So, as strange and new as their adolescent years are for *you*, just imagine what it feels like to *them*. Their bodies are changing, the social rules are changing, their emotions are sharper and sometimes frightening, sexual feelings are stirring, and their family relationships are changing. That is, you have company in being freaked out by the adolescent years. Even more frightening is the fact that so many of our teenagers' experiences are taking place out of our sight as parents. We don't see what they do, and we don't often hear what they do. They are out of the home more than any other generation and involved in more isolating activities when they are home.

So, here's the hard truth. Many of your worst fears about your teen will, or very well might, come true. Odds are that your teen will try pot, drink alcohol, have sex, cheat on a test, drive too fast, blow off a day of school, and do a number of other things that would surely not gain your approval. You cannot prescribe an immunity to the real world, no matter how cautiously or thoroughly you parent. Yes, many of your worst fears about your teenagers will probably come true. I just don't believe that these should be your worst fears. The teen years are not an end game, a final answer about character development, or a report card on your acumen as a parent. No, adolescence is a broad developmental step in the process of life, a critical period during which, through trial and error (often lots of error), character is established and developed. And each experience and misstep provides an opportunity for you to practice availability, to foster resilience, and deepen your relationship. Trust me, smooth waters rarely present such grand opportunity.

THE ADOLESCENT MIND

The cognitive changes brought on by adolescence are often difficult for the teen in transition to manage. A child who lags behind developmentally may suffer in school for the first time. With normal development, these children catch up with their peers, but we need to be aware that this transition can be quite a struggle and recognize our child's level of cognitive development relative to his peers.

Accompanying the cognitive changes of adolescence is an increasing sense of self-awareness. This sense helps teens to learn more efficiently than they did earlier in life. They are able to think and learn vicariously, such that they do not need to experience situations firsthand in order to understand them, a very important component of cognitive development. With this self-awareness, of course, children learn quickly to become more self-conscious as well. Young adolescents become acutely aware of how they present to other people. This is so important, as it allows them to hone the skill of reading social cues. They can then adapt and adjust their behavior to gain social acceptance and avoid rejection.

For many teens, however, self-consciousness creates a great deal of turmoil and heartache. A young man I worked with years ago suffered nearly crippling social anxiety as a result of self-consciousness. He would spend hours of his evening reviewing the social elements of his day, criticizing his performance with his peers. He would sometimes send texts to friends asking whether they felt his behavior was appropriate, or if anything he said or did during the day unintentionally offended anyone. He said he often felt like an "idiot" or a "dumb-ass." For this young man, managing his self-consciousness had nearly become a full-time job! Although this story represents an extreme, I tell it because these concerns are not at all uncommon among even the highest functioning teenagers. It is likely that some of these concerns ring familiar to you from your own teen years. Certainly you can assume that, for many, self-consciousness comes at a cost. I remember this boy telling me that he yearned for the ignorance of his "youth," when his most prominent concern was whether the Cubs would win or not. Typically, by the way, they would not.

SOCIAL *IN*-SECURITY

> "Everyone loves me. At least I think they
> do. I wonder what they'd think if they
> knew I hated myself."
>
> —KELLY, 16

You need to know that all adolescents are, at least at times, socially insecure. Appearances, attitudes, and apparent ease of conversation may betray this fact for some, but it is a fact across the board. It is the nature of their age. With ever-changing minds and bodies, adolescent insecurity is really no wonder. Despite what every textbook on adolescence states, I was not entirely sure this was a fact until I began to ask, and the teens were more than willing to talk. Teens feel insecure about their bodies, insecure about their intelligence, and insecure about their social acceptability and lovability. Thing is, your teenager, like many, may not show you this vulnerable side of himself. Many do exhibit overt insecurity, but many other teens appear to be cocky and even overly confident. Know that this is simply so much defensive bravado. This is a vulnerable time in your child's life. Knowing this, you can be sensitive to it despite appearances.

Most every teen I work with also tells me that he or she often feel lonely, despite the fact that many of them could not be busier with school, extracurricular activities, and the social scene. They all feel lonely at least some of the time, and often sad, too. Not necessarily cause for alarm, but certainly something that you as a parent should know. This is important because these emotions will not always be evident to you. In fact, many teens who feel sad and lonely present to their parents as angry, insolent, and difficult. Others may just disappear into their rooms with no indication whatsoever of how they feel. Recognize that your teen often may have other things on her mind, and she may not yet have developed a sense that "This too shall pass." Her social, academic, or emotional concerns may truly *feel* catastrophic to her, even if it seems to you that her issue is relatively insignificant. I encourage you to be cognizant of, and sensitive to, where your teen is developmentally. It will save you both from potentially serious miscommunication. I should note that, as a clinician, I become most concerned when the negative mind states are longer-lasting. Should they interfere with day-to-day functioning, professional help may be indicated.

BREAKING AWAY

Now, first and foremost, you need to know that developmentally, your adolescent is, by nature, highly egocentric. Yes, it's all about him! He is not yet expert at taking the perspective of someone else, including you. His *job* is separation and individuation, developing a sense of himself in the context of his relationships, and learning to cope with stress and manage his emotions. It is here, during adolescence, that your teenager learns self-motivation, self-starting, self-control, and frustration tolerance. He will also explore the trial-and-error method of experimenting with new things, and truly creative thinking. He may try different looks, linguistic styles, music, and so on. While traversing this terrain, your teen may seem difficult, irrationally emotional, contradictory, opinionated, and angry. If you pay attention, you will find that he can also be brilliant, insightful, and empathic at the same time.

In order to sustain your availability, and avoid replacing it with anger, disappointment, or dismay from *your* end, please remember that, in making her own choices and, yes, sometimes mistakes, it is not your teenager's purpose to test, torture, frighten, or confuse you, despite appearances. This is not her purpose at all. Rather, it is her *job* to establish a unique identity for herself and discover the type of person she strives to become. At this stage, your teen is deeply involved in her own story. I have found that it is often very difficult for teens to consider the impact of their actions on their parents at all. I do not mean to imply that they are incapable of doing so—it simply does not always come naturally to them.

On some level, teenage minds actively work *against* taking your perspective into consideration. They have been working from the foundation of your perspective, your values, and your timetables their entire lives. During the course of adolescence, they begin to develop their own values, interests, styles, and perspectives. To do so, they often try on different ways of being. You have probably seen this in your child, and perhaps written off these developmental steps as "phases." The label is less important than the fact that your teen needs to go through them in order to find himself and hear his own voice. So if you feel he's just being oppositional for the sport of pressing your buttons, recognize that the vast majority of the time, this is a normal and very important part of development. Choose your battles carefully here, as you want him to develop as freely, and safely, as possible.

Given all the emotional variables at play, many parents are naturally dismayed by the unpredictable and ever-changing moods of their adolescents. You may feel that, no matter what you say to him, it's somehow the wrong thing. One of the questions that parents most frequently ask me is "How do I handle my teenager's emotions?"

The answer is complex, because what we really want is to teach our teens to understand and manage their *own* emotions. As parents, though, we can play a role in kick-starting this process by asking open-ended questions in a nonjudgmental manner:

What is it that makes you so sad sometimes?

Why do you think you get so angry?

When are you happiest?

When are the toughest times for you?

In my experience, basic questions such as these, where we ask our teens to examine themselves objectively, are best asked at times of calm, not crisis. Keep in mind that many teenagers will not engage in this type of Q&A session at all, especially when first presented with the idea, and it will not serve you well to push them into it. Some things may be too emotional to discuss, and many teens are not very well versed in identifying their own emotions. Instead, I suggest simply making yourself available if they do want to talk about their emotions. Regardless of whether they ever take you up on your offer, they will be comforted knowing you are there for them. They may very likely forget to tell you so.

You can also serve as a role model and guide here, talking about your inner experience of your own feelings. So take the opportunity to talk with your teen about what life was like for you when you were a teenager. What made you anxious or insecure? How did you handle adversity? What were your relationships like with your own parents? By sharing parts of your story, you open a line of communication, and your teen may, at some point, relate directly or choose to share with you in turn. I encourage you not to consider talk about feelings to be simply touchy-feely and superfluous. The ability to label feelings, your own and other's, is the key to emotional intelligence, a major contributor to success in life. It is an important part of your relationship and a vital component of availability.

THE NATURE OF TEEN REBELLION

"My mom asked me the other day why I
fuck up. I told her the truth. I have no idea."

—MICHAEL, 15

Parents often ask me about teen rebellion—why it happens, and how long it will last. The most succinct advice on rebellion came from Jackie, mother of a 17-year-old girl. I told her about the concerns of some parents I had been working with. Specifically, I highlighted their fears that their younger teens were going to hate them for the duration of their adolescence, that their rebellious nature would endure. With her thick New York accent, between gum smacks, she offered the following nuggets of wisdom:

"Tell them not to worry too much about it. These kids, they grow, you know, they change. Adolescence isn't just the same the whole time. I mean, c'mon, right? Take my daughter, okay? She was rebellious for a while, first with me, then her father. But it was just a phase. It's much better now. My advice? Don't worry too much. Don't take it personally, but don't take any shit either! Oh, and save yourself some trouble. Just get unlimited texting and get it over with."

Sweet, profound, encouraging words, huh? Truth is, I could not have said any of it better myself, and so I quote. She's right. Adolescence is ever changing, rebellion tends not to last forever, and teenagers today text one another like mad. Don't kid yourself that your teen will be any different.

And availability *does* mean not taking it personally, and not taking any shit!

The adolescent need to separate from parents and foster a unique identity for themselves typically produces rocky results.

Separating from you may very well foster a certain rebelliousness in your teenager, a change in his look, new questions about your authority and household rules, and so on. Managing this rebellion on a day-to-day basis is a primary challenge for most parents of adolescents.

I should point out here that I tend to find myself more concerned with the teenagers who do *not* rebel and push back, those who are overly compliant with, or dependent upon, their parents. I have found that these teens experience the most difficulty in this process of establishing a unique identity for themselves. They are often anxious and insecure, in large part due to the fact that they effectively skip this separation/individuation stage. I find that arresting development in favor of compliance never works for the adolescent's sense of competence and well-being. So you can infer that if you have a difficult, button-pushing, argumentative teen, that's by and large a good thing. Tough for your short-term well-being, perhaps, but the right thing for your teenager's long-term development and success. Feel better? I know, I know, it's difficult.

SEX

As preparation for this book, I have perused a number of books on parenting adolescents. Most of them are stunningly brief in their discussion of sex, almost as if the authors sense the discomfort of the reader, gently assuring them, *Talk openly about it, share your values, but perhaps not your experience (ha!), and move on to something more benign, maybe homework or making the bed.* I have to admit, I had the same inclination. I told myself, I'll just say that sex is like drugs. Readers will be smart. They'll get it. Seems we're very hung up about sex in our culture, aren't we?

Well, we adults may have our hang-ups, but today's teenagers are actually, when asked, surprisingly *open* about sex. I think that they may be somewhat immune to the taboo because they are exposed to sexuality from so many sources at such an early age. Let's face it, many of our kids know more about sex at 14 than we knew years later. This openness may initially seem disconcerting, I know, but it also presents abundant opportunity for discussion. Most of us know by now that the toughest part of talking with our teen about sex is *our* anxiety, not theirs. And it's weird, talking to your kid about sex; I'll give you that. Seems like just yesterday they were into WebKins, Pokemon, and little stuffed monkeys that held on to pens. Maybe they still are. And now sex?! Quite confounding, huh? But we've got to put that anxiety to bed, so to speak. Kids know about sex and engage in sexual activity, more so now than ever. Teen sex is a reality. They need our ear and our guidance.

As parents, we'd be fools to ignore it.

Here's a bit of reality. The majority of kids have sex before their 20th birthday, more than a quarter by age 16. I have uncovered no single shred of evidence that teens who have sex *stop* having sex because their parents would like them to stop. Further, for this generation of teens, the language around sex is confusing as well. Hookups, for instance, can refer to anything from making out to intercourse, depending on whom you talk to and sometimes who's around when you're talking to them. Oral sex might mean sex, or it might be less than sex, and less taboo because one can continue to claim virginity with oral sex but not with genital sex. In some adolescent circles, social status comes from having sex with multiple partners, especially among boys. Others look down on those who have sex. Be curious: ask your teen what sex means to him and his friends, what the pressures are, and how he plans to respond. This is a great way to get started talking.

Oh, and to make things a bit more confusing, one study conclusively showed that teens lie like crazy about their sexual histories. In self-reports, boys tend to amp up the activity and numbers, presumably to seem cool. Girls are less predictable. Depending on the audience, they may over- or underreport activity to appear cool or chaste, respectively. Now check out this stat: Some data suggests that a parent who talks with a teen about sex may delay intercourse for up to two years. Okay, there's a little motivation for you. Get talking!

So what do you say, and how do you say it? I suggest a series of talks, not just one "birds and bees" bit like the *Father Knows Best* generation. I'm not sure how he did it, but my father got away with avoiding even this lame excuse for a talk. Since I never heard word one from either of my parents, my formal sex education effectively consisted of an anxious nun running a filmstrip for the fifth-grade boys in the chaste bubble of our suburban parochial school. I remember ovary diagrams, the word *vagina*, and *National Geographic*-type footage of animals. I can attest from experience that the bizarre trauma of viewing the shamelessly erect kangaroo penis never helped me once, not once, in my interactions with the opposite sex. In any event, we've got a different set of realities now, which require more active, and proactive, parental responses.

I suggest you start talking with your kids about sex earlier rather than later. Parents should be talking to their children about sex well before they become teenagers. If possible, you want to get the jump on the older brother or precocious storytelling classmate. I clearly remember Mike Costello, smiling broadly, dragging a dictionary to school in fifth grade, encouraging us to chortle wildly at clinical definitions for various organs and sex acts, all of us desperate to seem as if we knew our stuff. Today, an accidental Google search can take a preteen far deeper into the unedited abyss of sexual knowledge, with pictures and *everything*. Yeah, I think you'd better start having *the* talks sooner rather than later.

My personal preference is to match your first talks with the introduction to Sex Ed in grammar school. Now, you may not, of course, want to get into graphic detail with your fifth- or sixth-grader, who may very well be grossed out and embarrassed. But you want to open the discussion. Talk about the sex they see on TV. Ask about the Sex Ed at school. Just start talking. And keep talking. Remove the taboo of this type of conversation with your child, and she'll be more likely to talk to you, and listen to you, when it matters most.

The media provides nothing but fodder for these talks, as sex comes up every few minutes in just about every sitcom, reality show, and drama we watch. You may even clear up some fear or confusion in the process of talking. I had a session with a father and his 12-year-old son recently where sex was a frequent enough topic of conversation between them that it just seemed another agenda item in the meeting. This boy was perfectly comfortable talking with his father about sex, even joking about it. It was abundantly clear to me that this father's openness and availability would serve this young man very well through his teen years.

This does not, by the way, need to be dead-serious stuff. You can introduce some levity to the talk. When I first talked with my son about sex, we laughed about how weird it was that we were talking about sex. Which, quite honestly, made it okay. Regardless, if you have not yet started talking with your teen about sex, just start talking.

Once again, I'll quote Jackie. She had some strong opinions about how to address the topic of sex with teens. This sage, available mom agrees that we need to talk with our teens about sex, regardless of the discomfort. Our discussion went like this:

> *"She's having sex with her boyfriend. We talk, so she told me about it. I always make sure we have that kind of relationship."*
>
> *"But you can't be happy about this."*
>
> *"Hell, no, I'm not happy about it, and I told her so, but I wasn't gonna shut her out of my life for it. I love her, no matter what. I think she appreciates that I'm willing to talk with her about it. And I think it's because we talk that she demands respect from boys and practices safe sex."*
>
> *"Isn't it uncomfortable for you, though? Wouldn't you rather not know?"*
>
> *"No. That would be like...we had nothing, you know? This is better than not talking, for sure. I'd just be wondering every night otherwise, worrying about her. And I'd be suspicious, snooping through her stuff and asking questions. Oh, and I'd make my husband miserable! Believe me, I know that mom, and I do not want to be that mom!"*

She's so right. We've got to keep our heads out of the sand and talk with our kids about the things we most fear talking with them about, including sex.

I caution you not to judge yourself as a parent based on whether or not your teen is having sex. It is not "bad kids" who have sex. This type of judgment is the antithesis of availability and may drive our teens in all the wrong directions.

As parents, most of us, of course, do not condone sex between teenagers. If our child is having sex, it is not incumbent upon us to condone this activity. Quite the contrary, it is critical that our teens know how we feel and what our values are regarding sex. If they are already having sex, however, they are highly, highly unlikely to stop. And so we need to talk to them about our values, about loving relationships, about respect, about disease and safety. The least available thing we can do is to reject our teens for what they are doing. If your teen is sexually active, it is something he does. It may be foolish, it may be misguided, but I encourage you not to make it the sum total of your relationship with him. That is a recipe for a break in communication and hurt feelings all around.

When it comes to sex, we need to recognize that teens are people—they are flawed, and they're always learning. If you are available to your teen, you can be a teacher and a guide. You can have some impact on her behavior, because she will be open to considering your values in her decision making. If you are unavailable, you are simply perceived as an enemy. In the end, what parent wants that?

INTIMACY: MORE THAN HOOKING UP

Now, as parents of teenagers, I think we sometimes can get so caught up in our fears about sex that we forget about the underlying intimate relationship. We want to make sure our teens are home at a decent hour, before "it" is likely to happen. We want to make sure their dress is not too provocative. We make sure they are never alone in the basement together for more than a few minutes: "Don't mind me. Just changing the laundry." Yeah, we're good at this stuff.

Remember, though, that more often than not, the relationship your teen is engaged in is important to him. Many teens have shared with me that their boyfriend/girlfriend relationship has been a source of strength, joy, and even motivation in their lives. Bonus! Despite what we grown-ups may believe, recent research clearly indicates that teens take intimate and sexual relationships very seriously. This has proved to be just as true for boys as it is for girls, another serious blow to conventional wisdom. Also, intimate relationships between teenagers are not one-dimensional: good or bad, black or white. Teenagers use these relationships to *steady* themselves in a lot of ways. Often, these relationships contribute to their resilience in a number of areas.

Now, we need to monitor the boyfriend/girlfriend relationships of our younger teens, if we permit them at all, far more closely. We need to talk openly about not just sexuality, but intimacy, respect, and boundaries as well. In my experience, younger teens tend to "fall" so hard that they can become overly dependent on the relationship too soon. We need to recognize this phenomenon when it happens and encourage our teens to stay connected with others in their social circle. An available parent allows for ample open communication with a minimum of conflict here.

So I encourage you not to dismiss your teen's relationship as simply "troubling" or "distracting," as I have seen so many parents do. Talk to your teen about her relationship and what it means to her. We know that, in all likelihood, her relationship will end one day. If we are available to them through the duration of the relationship, we can serve as a resource and perhaps a shoulder to cry on when the relationship ends—another excellent opportunity for availability.

BODY IMAGE: THE LOCKER ROOM TERROR

> "Well, let's see. I hate myself. I'm fat and
> ugly. I'm revolting to boys. Other than
> that, I'm good."
>
> —COLLEEN, 17

We all know that the onset of adolescence brings significant physical, emotional, and hormonal changes. Most girls pass through the initial stages of puberty by 13, with boys lagging behind by as much as two or three years. We also know that many children reach puberty well ahead of the average, while many mature much later. There are taboos and concerns associated with both ends of the bell curve. I recently visited a middle school and happened to be trapped in the hallway between class periods. The variation among students in height alone was obvious and almost comical, but I was well aware of the emotional impact some physical differences can foster.

On an honest day, teens of all developmental levels, shapes, and sizes will admit that the locker room, and the showers in particular, are a source of particular horror for them. In fact, many of the teens I have worked with expressed a refusal to shower at school. Many others, concerned specifically about body image, have asked me to write notes pleading with teachers and administrators to excuse them from PE classes for "emotional reasons." I have heard stories about locker room bullying. Boys tend to tell stories about traditional types of bullying like getting "swirlies" and being stuffed half-naked into their lockers. Girls tend to share even more disturbing stories of verbal bullying: direct, blunt commentary on bodily flaws. Breast size, body fat, and the presence or lack of pubic hair are frequent targets. It is not difficult to envision the vulnerability so many teens suffer in locker rooms and showers.

I spoke recently with a pretty, petite high school junior who detailed her nightly plan for managing the locker room the following day because she did not want to tarnish her reputation as "attractive." She made sure she was in and out of the showers and dressed before the bullies, or anyone else for that matter, had an opportunity to see her. She often found herself panicking as she hustled through this process. She explained how adept she has become at covering up her slight belly and large hips with the proper clothing. All this work and planning, and this was a girl who believed that most of her peers found her to be *attractive*. Imagine what some other teens must suffer! It is critical that parents of teens be aware of the emotional dynamics that accompany these physical changes and challenges.

WHAT ABOUT THE GAY ISSUE?

Over the years, a number of teens have been referred to me in the wake of parental anxiety that they might be gay. In many of these cases, parents hoped I could get their teens to disclose the truth regarding their sexuality. The next course of action was rarely clear. Sometimes it involved acceptance, sometimes denial, often a nervous, huffy, "Well, we'll just have to talk about this, won't we?"

I learned a lot about this issue from a 15-year-old client, Peter. He and I were discussing the possibility that he might be gay. He stated, quite thoughtfully, it seemed to me, "I don't know. Maybe. What do you think?" He seemed unsure and curious, but not terrified. His parents, on the other hand, seemed terrified. When

I asked, they said quite honestly that they were fearful for Peter: "Won't life be so much tougher for him if he's gay? Won't he be mocked and bullied in school? Will he ever go to a school dance, or get married?"

In the end, it was clear that these parents knew and loved their son, regardless of the circumstance. It was about a year before Peter gained clarity regarding his sexuality, and his parents were open and available to talking about it.

Sexual preference and identity are important, dynamic issues. I have a friend who knew without question he was gay at eight years old. His mother accepted this about him immediately as fact, embracing his sexual preference as a part of who he is. Of course, parental feelings are not always so clear, or so supportive. As far as I know, my friend's father has denied his homosexuality for more than three decades.

Years ago, I worked with Elizabeth, whose mother accused her of being gay because she dressed so "butch" and never dated. Now, Elizabeth knew she was not gay, but she questioned openly what kind of mother would not *know* the sexual preference of her daughter, and would not choose to ask. She felt that, as far as her sexuality was concerned, her mother was distinctly unavailable.

So, regardless of your feelings about homosexuality, I feel strongly that your availability as a parent is critical if this is an issue for your teen. I've heard too often from gay teenagers that their parents are not interested in hearing about their feelings, let alone available to help them sort through them. I've been shocked to hear a few describe parents who call them names, effectively shaming them into silence regarding their sexuality. This seems a great way to create an impenetrable wall between a parent and a child.

Now, consider the alternative: availability. You are willing and open to talk with your teen about his sexuality and any feelings he may have of being different from his peers. You keep in mind that he is not a different person because he is gay. He has just gained clarity about his sexual preference. Honestly, I cannot think of a circumstance more rife with possibility for a deepening relationship with your teen, who is likely experiencing some of the same feelings as yourself: fear, confusion, maybe a sense of loss. Your teen needs your open mind and heart, your availability.

PART TWO

WHAT NEVER WORKS

"I respect my father. I love him, and I don't want to hurt him. But he doesn't believe in me, and I know it!"

—PAUL, 15

WHY LECTURES NEVER WORK

"Don't lecture me. That's always such a joke! I never listen to them when they lecture. Just because I'm looking at them doesn't mean I'm listening."

—CLAIRE, 16

The situation felt urgent. It was the middle of the day, and Mom asked for an "emergency session." She arrived promptly with her seventeen-year-old son, both clearly shaken. Dad arrived a few moments later, annoyed that the train was delayed. Decked out in suit and tie, he came armed for war.

Turns out his son, Sean, had been caught red-handed breaking into a friend's locker at school. The result: A three day suspension. This was day one.

Without fanfare, Dad began the lecture:

"Son, to me this is a matter of character. That's what bothers me the most here. You lack character. You take no responsibility for your actions, and I wonder what this reckless behavior will mean as an adult. I mean, can you function? Will you make it? Or will these character flaws keep getting the best of you? I just don't know. But I do know that we cannot keep going at this rate. Your mother and I, we're at the end of our rope."

"Well, Dad, I..."

"No! I'm talking, son. That's another thing. There's simply no respect from you. None at all. Where I come from, you couldn't treat people like that."

And on and on. Dad, a prominent attorney, filibustered for nearly an hour. Sean made an occasional attempt to chime in, express a modicum of remorse, or explain. But Dad was on a roll. He had a rapt audience, perhaps for the first time in a while, and he wasn't handing over that mic to anyone. Honestly, I don't blame him. Here's a guy who gets things done, who's so good with words, and he's desperate. This time, Sean was going to hear him out.

Well, the hour ended, and I was forced to dismiss this family, unceremoniously and without resolution.

Sean came in the following week, and I asked him to reflect on the emergency family session. Had he learned anything? Was he alarmed? Did he fear he had lost the good will of one or both of his parents?

"Oh, man, I barely remember. My dad just kept talking and yelling at me, right?"

"Um, yeah. You don't remember that?"

"Nah. That's, like, every day for me, you know? I tune out. He just has to have at me every once in a while. Plus he never asked me what happened, ever. Just yelled."

Lectures. When our kids slip off track, we're all drawn to lecture. Somewhere along the line, most of us have gotten pretty good at them. We can be angry and indignant and highly articulate when we're angry and afraid for our children. We can also come across as dull, disconnected, and redundant.

Remember, you did not just begin parenting this person. You have been teaching and guiding him for his entire life. He has learned. He knows you. In Freudian terms, you are his internalized superego—that is, his conscience is your implied voice in his head. So your teen knows the lecture. I have asked teens to take over the lecturing for their parents on occasion in my office, and they tend to do a remarkable job of capturing the essence of the lecture, often with admirable dramatic flair. Your point is already made, and your teen knows you care—despite what he says, he knows you care. I have worked with some exceptionally contentious family relationships, and I have yet to come across a single teenager who did not know that her parents loved her and cared about her. Of course, this has not always meant a peaceful coexistence, but you can trust that a foundation of love is there and is understood.

As there are exceptions to every rule, I feel compelled to add an additional note regarding lectures. I recognize that for some of you with more anxious teens the above advice may appear not to apply; you may feel that I'm all wet on this one. Your child is more than compliant when you lecture her. She takes direction well, and almost always does as she is told. The problem here is, her compliant behavior is a reflection of *your* competence. *Her* competence, on the other hand, remains unproved and untested.

The message she receives is that she needs to depend on you to lecture her and make decisions for her; ergo, you must believe that on some level she is incapable of doing so on her own.

The lecture doesn't work because it is a closed form of communication. There is no back-and-forth to it. I recommend instead open discussions, outside the drama and high anxiety of crises: "Listen, I've noticed lately that your grades have been slipping, and I'm really concerned. What's going on? How can I help?"

This would undoubtedly be a more effective opener than any lecture. And I suggest asking questions because, in my experience, we parents typically do *not* know what's really going on. For instance, there may be a number of reasons a teen's grades start dropping. We have to ask in order to understand.

Bob's Story

I was talking to my friend Bob, who told me a great story that illustrates effective parenting without lecturing. Bob recounted to me a brief moment with his mother back when we were teenagers. Now, Bob's mother was wheelchair bound at the time; Bob was responsible for physically carrying her up the stairs when she was ready for bed or when he got home for the evening. When we stayed out beyond our curfews, many of us had to guess whether our parents would be up waiting for us and whether there would be a price to pay. Well, Bob *knew*. His mom could not make it up to bed without him. One night, Bob was out with friends and, in his words, "tossed a few back." As usual, when Bob arrived home, his mother was waiting for him to carry her up to bed. Bob went to pick her up, and as he approached she got a feel for his wobbly stature, glassy eyes, and alcohol breath.

She looked at him and said calmly, "You're not carrying me anywhere."

That's it. No chastising. No prolonged guilt trips. No punishing. No rants. No long lectures on the nature of teen drinking. She knew that Bob got all he needed from those few words, and so did he. This event was never repeated as long as Bob lived under his mother's roof. He heard her, and his mother trusted in her parenting enough that she knew he got it. Now, Bob shared with me that he felt guilty that night, and he had to find a way to deal with that guilt. I trust that if Bob felt he needed to talk more about this event, he could have done so with his mother. But he never felt the need. By and large, they have a good relationship. Even as a teen, Bob enjoyed his mother's company.

Now think for just a moment about how this evening could have gone differently had Bob's mom chosen a less available approach. These are the moments that color parent–teen relationships. With each episode, parents have an option, and availability is always an option. We just need to slow our angry, fearful, ego-driven mind and allow ourselves to hear our intuition. Like Bob's mom.

What I haven't told you is that this episode took place almost 30 years ago. Bob recounted this tale as if it had taken place yesterday, and my hunch is that Bob's mother influences his availability with his own children all these years later. I've noticed that availability tends to have legs like this. It carries from generation to generation.

Finally, note that Bob's story is not about a handicapped parent. Quite the contrary, really.

WHY VICARIOUS LIVING NEVER WORKS

Parents living vicariously through their children: this is a frequent theme in my practice. I have worked with the father who is desperate for a legacy at his alma mater or in his fraternity, hoping to reclaim past glory. I know the mother who wants a perfect beauty queen for a daughter, wishing to heal the scars of her own unmet dreams. I have worked with parents who seem wholly unaware that their plan for the success of their child consumes them, becomes the focal point of their existence. Granted, vicarious living does not always play out in such clear and obvious ways. Regardless, it is something we parents need to hold in our lens of awareness.

One sneaky method parents often use to live vicariously through their children and teens is overscheduling. Many of us start this when our kids are young, when a typical week may combine soccer practice with baseball games, with swim meets and academic enrichment, between Suzuki violin and piano lessons. The number of activities may diminish a bit with the age of the child, but the theme is the same. Sometimes activities are the choice, and often the unfulfilled passion, of the parent, not the child.

The results can be pretty awful. One client of mine was a high school track star whose parents pushed her consistently. She excelled in the sport, earning a full scholarship to a very impressive university. Soon after she arrived on campus, however, she realized that running was never her passion and that the energy that got her to this point came almost exclusively from her parents. Once she was far from home, she could finally hear her own voice—and her desire to get off the track and try other things. Today, she resents her parents for forcing the sport on her, without ever checking in to see if it was what *she* wanted. Her parents, in turn, were angry themselves, because they had spent a great deal of time, energy, and money to make this dream come true. Imagine the damage control just a few moments of communication might have provided years earlier.

Another example: I worked some time ago with a nearly hyper-kinetically overscheduling family. My client, a 13-year-old girl, was involved in a shocking number of activities, including lessons on no fewer than three musical instruments and full participation in traveling teams for both swimming and soccer. She was a singer, dancer, and actress and was sometimes pulled from school to attend auditions. On top of all that, she spent weekends in a special religious education program as well as an extracurricular language program. She got up early every day, completing homework and practicing her instruments, and stayed up late due to practices and rehearsals. Her parents' expectations far exceeded the capacity of any child, and, predictably, their daughter became highly anxious as a result.

The conclusion that these parents were living vicariously through their daughter came easily. They both bragged to me regularly about her achievements and how proud they were of her. They brought her to therapy complaining that she was not willing to push herself hard enough. I remember struggling to mute my reaction, but I could not hold back in one early session:

> *"My God, folks! How much is one child equipped to take on? Your daughter is breaking her back trying to please you. You've already got her going day and night. You want her to cut out sleep as well?"*
>
> *"I'm sorry? Well, we actually think she can do better!"*
>
> *"You've really got to think about what you're doing*

here. Whose dreams are being realized with all this activity?"

"Her dreams, of course! This is all for her! Well, Dr. Duffy. I thought you were going to help us find her motivation. But it seems you just may not be the therapist for us."

Perhaps not. But they stuck it out for a while anyway. Not until we connected this girl's anxiety to her activity level did these "tiger parents" understand fully the damaging dynamic that was playing out in their family. Thankfully, not only were they willing to alter the dynamic for the sake of their daughter's health, they allowed her to select the two or three activities that most interested her. They put their egos aside, and for the first time in their daughter's life, they truly listened. These parents proved that we can draw availability from the depths of ego-driven, vicarious living.

WHY MICROMANAGING NEVER WORKS

Have you ever run across a parent who micromanages her child constantly? A few years back, I witnessed a mother who overdirected her son without pause. Rarely did more than a minute pass before she would discharge some duty or point out some flaw:

"Michael, stop hitting your sister!"

"Michael, apologize to all the adults for how loud you are!"

"Michael, tuck in your shirt. It's sticking out!"

Hearing her go on and on about his behavior just about drove me mad. Imagine what it was like for Michael. Michael is young, yet his anxiety is already palpable. There is nothing he can do right! Everything, everything he does elicits a negative response from his mother. His only vocal reaction would be an occasional, not particularly heartfelt "Sorry." On the rare occasion when she complimented him with "You're a good boy" or some such line, his reaction was no different than if she were admonishing him. He could never put words to it, but he in effect learned that his mother is unable to trust him with his own well-being. Not only is the potential for any feeling of competence taken from him, but his mother's micromanagement of his behavior also damages her credibility with Michael. Even at a young age, he does not know what to do with her, how to react. Furthermore, the microman-aging behavior Mom exhibits has far more to do with Mom and her ego than Michael, and I think this is true of most parents who micromanage. Sure, it's important to point out that the stove is hot—safety is an issue. There is not a whole lot at stake when a shirt is slightly untucked, however.

If you are a micromanaging parent, I strongly encourage you to look inside to determine what unmet need of yours is fulfilled by your micromanaging behavior.

Let's be clear here about one very important point. Your teen-ager will screw up. Your teenager should screw up. Your teenager needs to screw up in order to learn, to grow. Your job as parent is to provide a safe holding environment for this screwing up and learning to take place. You don't have to tell him how, or show him how. He'll have to figure that part out on his own, sooner or later. No, you just need to be unconditionally loving and avail-able so that he can fully and safely experience the strange, messy, perfectly beautiful journey that is adolescence.

We cannot overestimate how difficult it is for some parents to let go of the wonderful, bright, cheerful child out of whom their teenager sprang. I worked with a mom and dad recently who wept about the loss of that child as if they had truly lost her. We mourn these stages of our children's lives in different ways, all of which should be respected. Too often, though, this grief results in the infantilization of a teenager, making every little decision for them, micromanaging them, not allowing them to grow up and begin the work of adolescence. One mom recently admitted, after some chiding by her husband, that she laid out her son's clothes for the next day each evening, made her son snacks when he arrived home from school, and often performed his chores for him when he claimed to be tired. Her son is 17 years old! And in so many ways, he is still a child. In time, she recognized that she needed to let him go in order to let him grow.

Instead of choosing to see the loss of the child, I prefer to view the change toward adolescence with the same sense of amazement and wonder as any other passage in life. Your teenager remains that child, with all the accumulated experience and love and struggle, growing up into the remarkable young man or woman he or she is intended to be. I choose to view adolescence with awe, as an opportunity to develop a new kind of relationship with your ever-growing teenager. Seeing your adolescent through these eyes may free you from your grief, and allow you to experience a new set of more positive emotions about him.

And you can let go of the need to micromanage.

Insider Tip

Let me share with you one of the tricks of the trade for clinicians that I think will further alleviate your stress. When you come into my office and tell your story, discuss your problem, and describe your issue, I am interested and attentive. I want to understand, as best I can, your concerns from your point of view. I may take copious notes. Unless your circumstance is crisis-related, however, you should know that I am far more interested in your process than in the outcome. Generally, I want to see how you operate, how you go about solving problems, how you adapt and change.

Change is a process. Growth is a process. Allowing your teenager to screw up and learn—this is process as well. If we choose to rescue our teen from every potential pitfall, we unwittingly disrupt her process and take some critical opportunities away from her. First, we take away any opportunity for learning from the experience. We also take away the satisfaction and pride that come with a problem well solved. While we're at it, we take away her ability to prove her competence, both to herself and to you, the parent. In doing so, we give her the false impression that we will always be there to pick her up when she falls. We create a wholly unnecessary dependency. Now, this may provide us as parents with a role to play, parent-as-hero, but it robs your child of the opportunity to ever feel like a hero herself.

Early in my career, I too often worked under the misguided perception that my clients came to my office so that I might provide them with answers and solutions. In time, I learned that it is far more often my job to provide an environment where my clients can work through their process, talk through their issues, and solve them for themselves. In this way, I think my job nicely mirrors that of an available parent. As parents, we serve as vessels through which our children find their way. The sense of competence they experience when they do so for themselves is far, far more powerful than the experience of having a decision made for them could ever be.

To sum up, no teenager will welcome being imprisoned by rules that govern their every move. Micromanagement robs your teen of the ability to get into a little trouble, make some mistakes, and struggle a bit to find his way out of them. This is where he finds his competence, and we do not want to take away his capacity for competence, as long as safety is not a prevailing issue.

WHY SNOOPING NEVER WORKS

> "You do not need to know everything that
> goes on in my life. No. In fact, I promise
> you do not want to know everything that
> goes on in my life. That doesn't mean things
> aren't okay, you know? It's just that there's
> some stuff we should keep to ourselves, for
> everyone's sake."
>
> —CHRISTINA, 17

After reading the previous section, you may find yourself relieved that you are not one to micromanage. Well, don't be so sure. Through my work I have found that gathering data unduly, collecting "intel" on your child, is akin to micromanagement. Snooping through rooms, journals, Facebook, and last night's texts—these intrusions into the privacy of your teen are not the hallmark of the available parent.

Frequently, the therapy room is a confessional. I often hear from sheepish parents, most often mothers, that they have decided to peek into their teenager's journal or Facebook status to get a glimpse into their lives. I have never heard a parent say they were happy with what they read. More often than not, it is alarming. I have personally read a number of teen journals (only because, by the way, I was *invited* to read them). In one entry, I may read that a teen is so upset with her social life that she is thinking of killing herself. In the next entry, she may be angry about being mistreated by a parent or teacher. In another, she may feel great having connected with a boy. I do not minimize or dismiss any teen's feelings at any time. But you put yourself in a very tough situation when you read your teen's journal without permission.

First, you may find out a lot about your teen's life you did not want or need to know. You also have little context for interpreting what you see, which creates a fertile breeding ground for misunderstandings.

I worked with a dad recently who took his fifteen-year-old daughter's phone from her as he caught her texting past her bedtime. He really wasn't so angry, but he knew her phone was too enticing and stimulating for her to fall asleep. He cited his own experiences staring at his iPad well into the night, driving bouts of insomnia he did not want his daughter to suffer.

Well, curiosity got the best of him as he reached for his daughter's phone on the bedside table. He started reading her texts.

Ten sleepless hours later, he was in my office, exhausted and bereft. He had spent the entire night reading through every text, every single text, his daughter had ever sent or received. Suddenly, he felt as if he did not know her at all. He could not believe the language, the flirting, the suggestion of unspeakable misbehavior. Questions began to emerge: Was she having sex? Was she drinking? Doing drugs? Did I raise a bad kid, and she's just been fooling me?

Without context, I see why he wondered. He felt inconsolable, and the damage had been done. But if he had not read the messages, he would have felt no different about his sweet daughter. And she is a sweet girl. She was not having sex, or doing drugs. She is who he thought she was.

But she's a teenager.

Snooping is different today than it was a generation ago. Our teens are not passing notes that can be torn up, or whispering in halls. They leave a larger footprint, a more permanent, virtual footprint. And snooping there would be akin to our parents hearing every word we spoke as teenagers. Think about that. There are some things parents do not want or need to know or see. For that reason, I strongly encourage you to quash that urge to snoop.

And keep in mind, there is a world of difference between snooping and guiding our kids through this tricky world of texting, Instagram, Facebook, and other online landmines. We need to tell them, with clarity, that nothing they put out in that virtual universe is either private or temporary, so be careful. Kids get in trouble all the time posting or sending the wrong words, the wrong photos. The risks are enormous. I have worked with kids referred to me solely for what passed through their cell phone.

But snooping is different, and peeking parents are in a particular bind. Having read things they were not intended to know, they sell themselves out as snoops if they act on the information they learned. As a result of this quandary, what happens more often than not is that the parent does nothing, but worries more. Nothing solved or resolved, just more fear. Further, your daughter would of course consider it an enormous violation of trust if she were to discover you had peeked—and, of course, she would be correct. As you might guess by now, I believe talking with your teenager is a far more effective way to know her. It is a genuine, sincere, available approach. Get caught peeking, and no matter what you read, your violation of her trust will become the issue.

Now, updates on social networking sites like Facebook and and Instagram are a bit different. There is an element of public domain here. Inappropriate or overly revealing messages can *absolutely* present a safety issue, especially for younger children. As parents, we need to stay on top of this issue, as some children may not demonstrate the maturity or control required to be safe and responsible. I encourage you to be on your toes here. Trust your instincts to know when your child is ready, and keep an eye on your child's Facebook page. As far as I'm concerned, for the first couple of years, you should share her password so that you have access anytime. Even better, try what I do with my nieces and nephews: become "friends" with them. This way, you can be a watchdog when necessary, sure, but it can also be kind of fun.

WHY UNDERESTIMATING NEVER WORKS

> "You can take young people, who are relatively inexperienced, and expect enormous things of them, and they'll rise to the occasion."
>
> —RICHARD GRIFFITHS, ACTOR, HARRY POTTER FILMS

I worked recently with a teenage boy who was brought in by his parents to see me for delinquent behavior. He had vandalized some cars in the neighborhood and stolen some clothes from a local shop. His grades had also been steadily dropping throughout the school year. He had always been an A and B student, so this sudden change was rather troubling indeed. To make matters more upsetting, he had a superstar older sister, an athlete enrolled in a prestigious university and doing quite well.

At one point early in his treatment, this boy told me that his father had suggested that college might not be for him, that maybe he should consider the trades or a junior college. The boy was clearly shaken by the suggestion. He always assumed he was smart and would attend college like his sister. He expressed shock that his father's faith in him could be so easily broken, and he began to believe that he was truly limited, or damaged, that he could not be successful in college. He began to fear for his future and what would become of him if he could not find success. Parenthetically, I should note that this young man's delinquent behavior was in the end a call for help related to depression and suicidality. Often, with teenagers, things are nowhere near as clear and obvious as they may first appear: another indication that we parents need to limit our assumptions and allow ourselves to be fully present and available to really *hear*.

Now, when we underestimate our teenagers, the bar drops. They lower their expectations for themselves as well. This is evident in the example cited above. Availability in parenting does not mean *soft* parenting. Without reasonable expectations, our children lack a measuring stick for their own success. Keep in mind that expectations are only effective when they are reasonable. But I believe that every person has the potential to make a *great* contribution to the world. This is a major part of our job as parents, helping our teen identify his greatness, recognizing it in him and expecting it from him.

Of course, your expectation is not the same as pressuring him to do what you want him to do. An expectation of greatness tends to raise a teen up, not burden him. If there is burden attached, consider whether you as a parent are operating from a place of availability or from ego. High, reasonable expectations are critical to the successful emotional development of any teen. But in order for greatness to be fulfilled, your teen needs to follow *his* path.

That stated, teens are not mind readers. A friend of mine recently shared a story with me about her 14-year-old son. She told me her husband was angry that her son was sleeping in on a recent Saturday morning, instead of getting up and cutting the lawn. Keep in mind, this obligation was never shared with the 14-year-old. Noon eventually rolls around, and said son rousts himself sleepily from his room. Throughout the day, he is greeted with grunts and criticism by his father, but he is never told about the lawn issue.

Finally, in the evening, this boy lets his mother know that he has been upset all day because his father seemed angry and incommunicative, and he has no idea why. Both father and son wasted an entire day being upset because of the lawn. The lawn!

The point is, as available parents, we cannot expect our children to read our minds. We need to communicate with them about what we expect. If those expectations are not met (14-year-old son fails to cut lawn after Dad requests that he do so within a certain time frame), it is reasonable to engage in a discussion about why the work was not completed. Teenagers are remarkable, but they cannot read minds. Talk to them. Let them know what you expect. It will work a lot better—promise.

Never underestimate the potential of your teenagers. They are capable of more than we can imagine, limited only by their own minds and your faith in them.

CHOOSING YOUR WORDS:
THE MAKING OF A 97-POUND WEAKLING

There is a stealthy little method parents use to damage their children's sense of self-worth. Chances are, most of us are wholly unaware when we do it. Be aware of the insidious little comments you might make about your teenager. Be aware of that fine line you cross between a good-natured joke and a damaging message that becomes a lifelong part of your child's script, the ongoing self-talk dialogue in his head.

When I was young, I was tall and quite thin. My nickname was "John Bones," and the joke in my family was, in effect, that I was not very physically strong. Once, when I was about 15, my father took me into the basement to show me how to lift weights, but it happened only once. Because it was not repeated, I took it to mean that I was hopeless in this regard, and my weakness was just woven into the family shtick, or routine. I carried this belief about strength with me for decades until I began to work hard to replace this part of my script in the past few years. Thing is, it was hurtful and limiting, especially in my teen years. I did not believe in myself, especially physically. The most disheartening part of this story for me is that, in retrospect, I was perfectly strong and capable as a teen. I was an okay athlete but, lacking faith in myself, I was cautious and fearful, a direct result of my family's influence. Because of this fear and the potential for embarrassment, I was robbed of the opportunity for self-mastery. Now, I do not think it was ever my parents' intention to make me feel incompetent in this way. This stuff is sneakier than that—over time, it creeps into the script of a family. Please be very aware of your words and the shtick you develop with your child. Chances are, your child is all but unlimited in what he can do. Allow him to stay that way.

WHY BLINDERS NEVER WORK

"Accept the facts when I tell you the facts.
Oh, and it won't always be what you want
to hear."

—BEN, 16

Too often, we decide what we want to hear from our teenager and what we want to believe about our teenager. This is understandable. Take, for example, the parent who claims, "Not my baby" when a group of teenagers is arrested for drug use. That mom does not want to believe that her son could be involved in such a thing. This makes sense. What parent would want to believe anything different? The problem arises when we ignore the truth, especially when it is right in front of us and obvious. I've seen too many situations where teenagers have to develop symptoms of depression or anxiety, these classic cries for help, in order to be heard by their parents.

In fact, I have seen several situations like the following in my practice. A teenager is feeling distress for weeks or months. He withdraws socially or hangs out with an entirely different crowd. He begins drinking or taking drugs. His grades plummet. His parents recognize the change, but write it off as growing pains, adolescence in general, or maybe getting accustomed to a new school or grade level. Mom and Dad take meticulous care selecting punishments for each "infraction," and they let their son know they are disappointed and expect better of him. They feel as if they are doing what they need to do to stem the tide of negative behavior. Somewhere along the line, a crisis develops. Often, in my clinical work, the crisis involves a suicidal gesture or related thoughts. This is typically when parents finally "hear" their teenager: *Ah, there's a problem. He feels sad, frightened, or hopeless.* Then the mental health brigade is called upon to seal things up and make it better. In my experience, this is also the point at which the parents begin to question themselves: *Where was I? Why didn't I notice what was really going on? Why did I not do more?* Guilt and shame often drive the answers.

Let me be clear here. I am in no way condemning these parents. By any standards, these are good, caring, intelligent people who truly love their teenagers. My point is to illustrate the degree to which even focused, aware parents can miss the boat when it comes to their teenagers and their lives. Now, I recognize that suicidal behavior or thinking is not requisite for most of us to take notice that something is amiss in the lives of our teens. But the nature of the crisis is a matter of degree, and as parents we have methods available to us to prevent these circumstances. The two most important are attending and listening: removing those blinders.

By way of example, the Office of National Drug Control Policy recently launched a campaign directed at parent naïveté regarding adolescents as part of an antidrug program. Based on extensive survey data, ONDCP found that 80 percent of parents believe that drugs and alcohol are not available at the parties their teens attend. Eighty percent! What, do we not *remember*? Come on, people!

The good news here is that most teens will talk about this stuff—sex, drugs, and so on—if asked. In my experience, a surprising percentage of today's teens are open and honest when asked about almost *any* issue. But chances are, you've got to ask—rare is the teenager who initiates this type of talk. Further, you need to be prepared not to hear exactly what you would like to hear. Still, I think teens are more open and honest today than we were a generation ago. What a great opportunity for the available parent!

After all, isn't it better that you know the reality, so that you can guide your teen toward healthy, safe decision making? Please do not make the mistake of choosing to remain in the dark when it involves the reality of your teenager's life. A little discomfort is a small price to pay for your knowledge and your child's safety. Further, discussions around these tough topics provide fertile ground for fostering your relationship. Feeling the discomfort and starting the talk anyway—this is the way of the available parent.

Still, I can fully understand how the "Not my baby" syndrome might infect a family. Like many teenagers, my client Andrew took his first drink at 15, experimenting with alcohol along with three of his best buddies at the time. Within just a few months, Andrew's behavior changed dramatically. He suddenly dressed in all black. He quit the football team. His grades plummeted. He abandoned his friends in favor of a completely different crowd.

Andrew's older brother Chris was away at college during this time. In a family session, I learned that the change, which seemed somewhat gradual to his parents, was quite shocking to Chris. Between the end of summer and Thanksgiving break, Chris reported, Andrew became a completely different kid. He said he heard rumors from friends still in high school that Andrew was quickly gaining a reputation as quite the partier, getting drunk or high nearly every night. Chris was so angry with his parents about the change. He said they did not seem to notice or be concerned. When Chris asked, his mother replied that adolescence was simply different for Andrew. In other words, "Not my baby."

Turns out, Andrew was on a downward spiral into addiction and depression that would last years and threaten his life on more than one occasion. I frequently wonder how things might have been different if Andrew's parents had recognized and accepted the severity of the situation earlier, instead of insisting that everything was fine—not because they were bad or negligent parents, but because they so wanted it to be true.

I encourage you to see the writing on the wall. Don't expect your teen to come to you to tell you he is in trouble. He may very well not know. If you see dramatic change, act on it. Seek help. Don't believe him if he tells you everything is fine but your intuition tells you differently. The available parent is worldly, wise, open, and perceptive. You know better than anyone when your child needs help. When these circumstances present themselves in your family, engage in the tough talks, ask the tough questions. You will earn his respect, and better ensure his safety. Make yourself available as an instrument of assistance by lovingly acknowledging the possibility: "Perhaps my baby."

WHEN TO ASK FOR HELP

You may face crises during your child's adolescence that you feel are well beyond your breadth of knowledge and resources as a parent. You may find that your teen is using some drug excessively or seems suddenly or significantly more depressed. She may stop communicating with you or express that she feels a level of anxiety that makes it hard for her to get through the day. You may discover some other mental disorder or profound emotional issue or behavior, such as cutting, an eating disorder, or suicidal ideation. Any of these issues would indicate a referral to a mental health professional. None of them, by the way, signal failure on your part. Quite the contrary, by consulting with professionals when needed, you are profoundly available and using every resource at your disposal to ensure that your child is safe and that her well-being is tended to.

I further encourage you to be available as part of the healing process. A therapy room is not Jiffy Lube, a place to drop off your broken teenager to be fixed. Deepen your relationship by working through tough times together. Believe me, the darkest of times can provide the brightest opportunities to get to better know and understand your teenager.

Other parents can also be an excellent source of help in difficult times. To calm her anxiety about her daughter entering adolescence, a mother in my neighborhood came up recently with an excellent idea. She planned a Q&A session with myself and other parents in the area, a de facto support group to discuss the issues of oncoming adolescence. I strongly encourage you to seek the support of other parents in some way if you find yourself overly worried about your future or present teen. I also encourage you to talk with teenagers. They'll typically share the realities of this time of life with you, sometimes quite bluntly, but they may also dissipate some of your fear. If you have a specific concern, look for a Parent University in your area. These are daylong miniconferences, lectures, and seminars that typically take place at high schools. Chances are, if you have a specific concern or challenge, there are other parents who share it.

WHY JUDGING NEVER WORKS

So, Dr. Duffy, what are we supposed to say and do if our teen is hanging out with the wrong crowd? What if we don't like her boyfriend? What if we don't approve of the way her best girlfriend dresses? What are we supposed to do then? Well? Huh? Huh? Good questions. Glad you asked.

As parents, we have these gut reactions, don't we, to our children's friends, peers, and potential boyfriends and girlfriends? Most parents I have worked with act on this by blurting out their distaste: "Who are her parents, and do they know she's wearing that out in public?" Or "That boy has a severe attitude problem." More often than not, if they get a bad vibe from a particular teen, or they hear rumors that the kid is bad news in one way or another, parents will forbid their child from ever being with said kid. I'm conducting a survey, and I want to hear from you: In the history of adolescence, including your own, has this tactic ever worked, even once, in keeping one teenager away from another? Has it ever fostered anything other than anger, defensiveness, and noncommunication? No. We all know how this goes. Once a friend is forbidden, they are the first to get a text message from your kid. A clandestine meeting is arranged. They become the best of friends, bonding over their rebellion and the ongoing drama of their relationship. To top it off, you, being the forbidder in the first place, are officially out of the loop. The way you have written this drama, you are now the enemy. You are avoided, lied to, danced around.

Perfect.

This one is tough. I suppose, for many of us, it would be handy if there were a loophole in this availability concept that allows us to be judgmental, as long as it's about someone else's kid. That would make it easier. Alas, there is no such loophole. Availability is an all-or-nothing deal.

I also realize that I can't ask you to just sit on your hands on this one either. No, I think if we have a negative vibe about a friend or potential boyfriend or girlfriend, we need to make our feelings known, but my experience with families tells me there is really only one way this works effectively. We need to do it in the context of an open conversation. Sit him down and ask about his new friends in a nonjudgmental way. Let him know your concerns. Stay away from judging phrases like the ones quoted above. And don't mandate that he stop seeing certain people. We already know how terribly ineffective this can be.

Perhaps toughest of all, be prepared to be wrong. This is big. I have come to believe that there is no such thing as a bad kid. Really. I have worked with some teens with terrible reputations who turn out to be wonderful, caring, sincere people. Perhaps they've made some poor decisions—*undoubtedly* they've made some poor decisions, maybe lots of them. After all, bad reps usually have some basis in reality, right? Still, I encourage you to truly listen when your child tells you about her peers. Don't just give her lip service while waiting to make your point. Your teen may even recognize some of the poor decisions her friend has made, and offer reasons she admires her anyway. Listen to her. Chances are, she is telling you the truth. Your teen does not just select friends to test your parenting skills. Being human, like you and me, she is probably choosing to hang out with people because she *likes* them.

I further encourage you to befriend your teen's friends. I have never known a better method for diminishing fear about *anyone* than getting to know them. This is where you will frequently learn that first impressions can often be so wrong. Invite your teen's friends over, or out to dinner with the family. Talk to them.

Be open to the possibility that you will like them, that you will identify unforeseen positives in their character and personality. Actively look for it. And keep in mind, there may be fringe benefits to getting to know your teen's friends. I've heard a lot of parents say that they learn more about their teen's lives from the friends than from their children themselves. Believe me, some of the most profound sessions in my office take place when a teenage client invites a friend to join us. Being open and available to your teen's friendships is part of being available to your teen. And remember, blaming friends for all of your teen's difficulties can easily cause a slip into the "Not my baby" syndrome.

Now, if discussion of friendships is enveloped in a cloak of availability that defines your relationship, such that your teen knows you are speaking out of love, concern, and trust, this can be a most effective, impactful conversation, an opportunity for growth in your relationship. This is not to say that your child will follow your advice and refrain from hanging with the bad-news kid. He might, he might not. But he will have *heard* you, which is more important. He will recognize your concern. He may be more vigilant around this person. You will have voiced a concern that allows him to make his own, better-informed decisions. The caring quality of your intervention, and the fact that you trust him to make good decisions, will empower him in future decision making as well. He will learn more about socializing, about human nature. Remember, you have raised him. He knows your values. He shares the majority of them, and he is equipped, given the opportunity, to decide for himself.

Yes, of course, he may mess up. He will and he should mess up, sometimes. He may realize he was wrong about that girl, and you were right all along. He may find that this new guy he's hanging out with is too reckless and self-destructive, taking risks your son is not willing to take. Talk to him about it, but don't rub it in. There's no need. He will have learned an important life lesson. Your forbidding contact between them is no substitute for actually experiencing the dynamics of other people in the real world. This is how we learn about people, about relationships. This is how we grow.

Of course, parental judgment does not fall solely on other children. We judge our kids as well. And in all likelihood, we judge them a lot. We judge them for their lack of effort, the music they listen to, the poor grades they receive, the clothes they wear, the money they spend, the bad choices they make that we would never have made when we were their age, what they eat, drink, smoke, watch, or send. Oh, yeah, we judge. I find that the only people anyone judges more often than themselves are their children. And teenagers know full well when they are being judged by their parents.

I want to be clear about the difference between constructive criticism and judgment. The former comes from a place of calm guidance in us. It is all but instinctual to reach out and help our child when we feel she is making an error, or that she will regret a certain behavior, or non-behavior.

Our judgment, on the other hand, tends to be derivative of our fear. We are afraid of what might happen to our child, of course. But we are afraid of what other people might think as well. We are afraid of failing as parents, or afraid to be seen as failures.

Judgment is neither helpful nor progressive. It is, unfortunately, an end point. It shuts down communication. It is destructive. The available parent guides, but she never judges.

No One's Watching

I often hear that character can be defined as what we would do if no one were watching. I like that. It's tough for us as parents, because our children are, to an extent, a reflection of us. A couple years back, I worked with a mom and dad who discovered that both their son and daughter were selling pot to their friends at school. A host of emotions followed for them, none more severe or vibrant than shame. They were worried about their children, of course. But they were also concerned, understandably, about their own reputations. How would others evaluate them? Would they be seen as bad parents?

This was embarrassing, and as far as they were concerned, everyone was watching.

We want to be proud of our children. We want them to be accomplished. We like to see their name in the paper when the honor roll is listed. We want them to score the winning run. We want them to make good choices. We want them to be admirable. And if we're honest, we want to feel admired for raising them.

But I'd like you to consider for a moment how you would parent differently if no one were watching, and if you were not concerned about others judging you for your parenting.

Would you feel freer? Would you address your child differently? In my experience, these are important questions to ask. I think we make better parenting decisions when they are unclouded by ego-based fears.

It's way more important than whether anyone's watching.

Why Smothering Never Works

> "I get more of my chores done around the house when she's not there, nagging me. When she's there, she hovers."
>
> —Ethan, 15

Another risk we run when we become overinvolved and personally overinvested in the lives of our teens is smothering them. Hovering parents, often referred to these days as "helicopter" parents, insist on spending way too much time with their teenage children. I have worked with teens who spend not only weeknights at home with Mom and Dad, but most weekends and weekend nights as well. In my experience, this phenomenon always comes from a very caring, sincere place in a parent's heart. "Time spent together builds strong families," I have heard. Parents have told me that they arrange their family lives this way to protect their teen from drinking, drugs, drunk drivers, bullies, all the threats of the outside world.

You certainly know by now that I am in favor of families spending time together. But teenagers need room to breathe, time with friends, time to explore their worlds, time to screw up, time to figure it out and grow. You are going well beyond availability if you insist on your teen spending all her free moments with you.

The results can be more troubling than you may at first think. I have worked with smothered teens who are ill-prepared to deal with the world outside the cocoon of home. Socially, they are not ready for the myriad decisions they need to make when first away at college, which becomes a failed experiment for many. They have trouble making and keeping friends, due in large part to their lack of experience reading and understanding social mores and cues. Their self-development can be rather severely stunted by the lack of experimentation in their lives. Honestly, these are the kids I worry about the most, those who are stuck in childhood, whose experiments in life take place only with Mom, Dad, and siblings. They tend to be insecure, anxious, and fearful, entirely unsure of themselves. They end up in therapy far too often. If you are a parent who holds on too tightly, I strongly encourage you to consider what need smothering is fulfilling in *you*. Consider also whether you are really helping to fulfill *any* need of your teen. Chances are, loosening your hold on your teen will allow him to find his own way. And trust me, it is never too late to change a maladaptive habit.

The mother of a 15-year-old boy recently shared the following thoughts with me:

> *"The hardest thing for me is watching him go out the door. I don't know exactly what is out there for him. I know I can't control it, but a part of me really wants to. I also know he needs to go, to do, to be. What would become of him if he didn't stumble and fall once in a while? He would never discover who he really is. Nothing could be scarier to me than that."*

And she's right, isn't she? You need to trust your parenting. But you need to trust your parenting, and your teen's judgment, in order for them to make it out there in the world. For a teenager, competence cannot be established in a vacuum.

So, to you smothering moms and dads out there, let 'em go, man! Give 'em a little push out the door if you need to. They can't grow if they're not out there. Believe me, they're ready and waiting. And no, your availability does not require smothering. Period.

WHY CODDLING NEVER WORKS

"My mom still makes my lunch, yeah. What? She's a mom!"

—LUCAS, 17

Coddling is among the worst things we can do to our kids. Remember the mother who continued to make the bed and choose the clothes for her son well into his teen years? I recall her implying that coddling defines a good, attentive parent. I understood what she meant. She felt, quite honestly, that she was taking care of her son, that this was her duty for as long as he lived within her jurisdiction. This, she felt, made the boy happy. When I looked at him sitting on the couch next to her, he seemed happy. Happy like a smug fox.

There is a very important reason that coddling doesn't work for our children. It is those little tasks, like making your own bed in the morning, that provide you with a sense of competence. We have to do something, accomplish something, in order to feel good about ourselves. Self-mastery and self-esteem are not birthrights. We earn them. We feel them when we complete a workout, cut the grass, close a sale, accomplish any job well done. Our teenagers gain a sense of competence when they experience success socially, do well on an exam, master a song on an instrument, or beat their best time in a race. An accomplishment does not need to be enormous to instill competence. Even incremental accomplishments can contribute to a positive sense of self-worth.

Now, your teenager may tell you they do not need this feeling of competence and confidence in themselves and their ability to successfully manage their world.

Don't believe them.

Don't believe that they are content just partying. Don't believe that just hanging out playing video games or talking to friends online does it for them. We all need that sense of accomplishment, of competence. Your teenager is no exception.

The rub is that many teenagers *claim* not to care about these things. I have heard the argument "I will never use geometry again, so why should I bother?" in my office ad nauseam. This, of course, is not the point. We don't have to love school for it to feed our self-esteem. Think about it: very few teenagers love school, but those who do their schoolwork tend to have higher levels of self-esteem. We simply feel good about ourselves when we do our best, regardless of what activity we're engaged in.

Instead of coddling, available parents provide opportunities for accomplishment, for self-esteem to flourish.

WHY OVERINDULGENCE NEVER WORKS

> "My dad is such a pain! He thinks I should have to drive some regular-ass car like him. No way! I want a Porsche!"
>
> —PETER, 17

A separate, but related, maladaptive parental behavior involves overindulgence. Years ago, I worked with a family who described a highly chaotic household. Accompanying the parents was a teenage daughter, Courtney, who was argumentative and noncompliant, yet seemed somehow lost as well. As bitchy as she was, and she *was* bitchy, I felt for her immediately. Within the first session, the familial pattern became evident. When I asked about curfew for this 16-year-old girl, her father told me, in no uncertain terms, that she stays out as late as she likes, with whomever she likes, "because she wants to." Despite major financial problems in the family, Courtney received a sweet new car for her birthday "because she wanted it." At the time, her parents were sharing some lame old beater. This girl had no chores around the house because, you guessed it, "she did not want to do them." Over and over, the parents took turns explaining their reasons: "Because she wants to," "But she'll be upset," "Because she told me to," "Because she says so." I had never seen a teen with so much *apparent* power.

Needless to say, this situation left me fuming. First, I found myself angry with Courtney, taking advantage of her hard-working parents that way. Shame on her! I soon realized, however, that she was only doing what her parents had taught her to do. They had taught her to be demanding, self-indulgent, and overly entitled. She was simply feeding off the behavior of her parents, following their lead. In addition, the parents would argue openly about Courtney right in front of her, one-up each other in the gift-giving department, and blame her troubles on each other's parental incompetence.

It does not take a therapist to see how the overindulgent behavior of these parents contributes to, and probably defines, the emotional and logistical chaos of the family. In this particular situation, Mom and Dad were masking marital problems with their overly indulgent parental behavior. Clearly, it was *their* issue that created the problems, not their daughter's. Courtney was the red herring, the perfect distraction for her parents' troubled relationship. If this dynamic plays out in some way in your family, investigate the origin of your overindulgence. It will serve as a guide toward helping you correct the pattern.

Courtney's parents would likely have argued that they were

indeed available, more than available, to their daughter. But by removing and decreasing expectations, by eliminating responsibility, they were actually depriving her. They were not depriving her of a new car, free time, or unlimited minutes. What they did deprive her of is the ability to develop her own sense of competence, and that's big.

"COOL" PARENTS:
THE STRUCTURE-FREE HOUSEHOLD

Believe it or not, your teen needs and wants structure and discipline. Those parameters provide a template for boundaries he will use throughout his life. Now, most teens are wholly unaware that structure and discipline constitute any part of what they need. I suspect that the teens who are aware that they need structure are too smart to tell you to your face. It's easier to keep quiet and get what they want right now—freedom, an iPhone, a day off school, the car keys.

Most will never tell you, but some will.

I recently coached a 17-year-old girl, Lisa, who told me about her nearly unlimited freedom at home. Her story is a lot like Courtney's. Lisa stays out as late as she likes, literally, both during the week and on weekends. She is allowed to have boyfriends in her room, door closed, no questions asked. She is allowed beer at home. There is in fact a fridge-full in the basement. Lisa and her friends have unlimited access; there is a "don't ask, don't tell" policy in the household. She is not accountable for her homework, and acknowledges the fact that she does just enough to get by in school—lots of C's, more D's. In effect, Lisa has been granted the ultimate freedom so many teens claim they want so badly. Hers are those elusive "cool parents," legendary in teen circles.

Now, I should tell you that Lisa is a highly intelligent, bright, articulate girl. She knows full well that she is capable of straight A's without breaking much of a sweat. She quit gymnastics at the onset of high school because she complained it was too much work. Her parents happily indulged her. Now Lisa tells me she wishes they had pushed her more, expected more of her. She feels her parents don't really believe in her ability in any way. In Lisa's mind, they've given up on her, so they might as well throw in the towel and let her have her way on just about everything.

This girl, this *teenager*, went on to tell me that she wishes there were some discipline in her life, some boundaries. When she came home recently at 2:00 A.M. on a school night, she knew her parents would not react. She's even come home "falling down drunk" and there's no punishment. When a boy left her room in the middle of the night, nothing happened. She laughs and says, "I wonder what it would take for me to get their attention! Do I have to set the house on fire?"

There is an enormous difference, I assure you, between being the "cool" parents, who look the other way and allow their teens to do whatever they like whenever they like, and being available parents. Listen to this girl. Lisa has every freedom most teenagers *think* they would like, but she knows she is not being parented. She knows she is missing out on some of the most critical, important lessons in life. If your own children never tell you, listen to Lisa.

In this same discussion, Lisa made another point that really struck me. She said her parents, and many of the parents of her friends, choose to be naïve to the activity of their teenage children. "They have no idea what we do. Most of us are drinking, a lot of my friends smoke pot,

> a couple girls have had sex. Our parents are idiots. They either have no idea what's going on, or they just don't want to see what's right in front of their faces." Sounds like the "Not my baby" syndrome. It can be lethal.

WHY BRIBERY NEVER WORKS

"Now my parents are paying me for grades.
Makes me feel like a loser."

—JANE, 15

Overindulgence can take other forms as well. I have worked with at least half a dozen situations in which parents effectively bribed their teenagers, quite handsomely I might add, in return for some behavior. Typically, this would involve a teen whose grades were poor or slipping. "Five hundred bucks per A, two-fifty per B" or "A new car if your GPA is higher than 2.5." These are real examples, I swear to you. In my experience, this type of bribery simply does not work. I must admit, the first few times I was confronted with it, I thought it would work for sure. Who wouldn't work a little, just a *little*, for a new car or a ton of cash? Come on, kid, a brand new *car!*

But, of course, when cooler heads prevail, it makes sense in the context of availability that bribery never seems to work. First, the natural consequence of any action, a failing grade, for example, is far more effective than any parade of bribes could be. Also, in the cases that I describe above, bribery was ineffective because the bribe did not address the core issue for these teens. In fact, I believe this type of bribery is incredibly shortsighted and actually supports teens' worst fears about their parents' belief in their competence.

Bribery, it turns out, is simply an ineffective, stopgap measure, a show of no-confidence that your teen can be successful of his or her own accord. And teens *get* this. This is the message they hear. So inevitably, if your teen is sabotaging his academic success one semester, he will not come through with better grades just because there is a car on the line. It just does not seem to work that way. I suppose that there are instances in which such a bribe will elicit the requested behavior, but the message your teen hears will be the same: "You don't believe I can do it on my own."

So even if it "works," it won't work.

Rather, the available parent talks with his teen about his slipping grades. Because the available parent has built up a sizable balance in the Emotional Bank Account, his teen is willing to talk with him. Parent and teen can problem-solve together. You may want to take her out to dinner when she does well, but please, take my advice and skip the bribe. In effect, bribery doesn't work because it is a reflection of unavailability.

Be aware of your own overindulgent behavior. Be aware of doing too much for your child, or giving too much to your child. Just be aware. Giving them *stuff*, material or otherwise, often deprives them of the most important of life's lessons, the ability to prove themselves, to themselves. There is *no thing* that can take the place of that.

WHY "GOOD COP, BAD COP" NEVER WORKS

"My mom's easier on me, no doubt."
—EDDIE, 15

Simply put, it is critical that both parents, if they are currently participating in their teenager's life, be on the same page on issues of importance. Teenagers are cunning in ways we parents can only imagine. If Dad is always soft and Mom consistently harsh, you can bet that Dad will be favored, first to be asked the big questions: "Can I stay out an hour past curfew?" "I'm so tired! Will you please call school and tell them I'm sick today?" "Can I go out now and finish my homework when I get back?" If these questions consistently flow to only one parent, it will not only cause animosity in your relationship parent to parent—nobody wants to play the bad cop all the time—it sends a terrible message to your teenager. First, he knows he can manipulate you, or at least one of you. He also knows he can pit you against each other. This phenomenon also creates an unbalanced situation in which one parent receives communication, but it is too often at the expense of the other. None of this contributes to a healthy dynamic in a family, and I strongly encourage you to avoid the "good cop, bad cop" drama at all costs.

It is especially important that parents speak with one voice during conflict. When tensions run high, your teenager will be confused by mixed messages, and he may just choose to hear the one he likes best in that moment. I have heard firsthand from teenagers the anxiety that comes from witnessing such conflict, hearing your parents arguing about you, disagreeing about what to do with you. Believe me, it is absolutely distressing and dismaying to a child to hear such talk. Clear it up and negotiate your differences as parents calmly and privately. When you are a united front, you can be available as parents. Disunity entirely discredits your availability.

For these reasons, it is critical that you talk to each other as a team about how you want to parent your teen, regardless of the nature of your relationship—married, divorced, separated, struggling. You cannot guide your children appropriately from *different* guidebooks. If you do, you are not giving your teen what she needs to make good decisions, and you are modeling poor decision making in the process. Talk to each other, often, about how you parent. You should discuss all rules, including curfew, chores, drugs and alcohol, safety, and allowable language and agree on your parenting methods privately. This is critical.

THE DAD CHALLENGE

A couple months ago, I gave a lecture on available parenting to a group of parents in a local high school auditorium. The audience was awesome: attentive and participatory, asking great questions, presenting unique parenting quandaries, and discussing clever solutions. But as I spoke and listened, something was nagging at me. About halfway through, it hit me.

There were no dads.

More than 100 parents in the audience, and not a single dad. I stopped cold, and pointed this out to the crowd to gauge their reaction.

The consensus was clear, and a bit surprising. Many of the moms present indicated that, despite the fact that gender roles are changing with time, they feel primary, sometimes sole, responsibility for parenting. Several said that they actually felt judged by their husbands when their children misbehaved, or performed poorly in a class. Somehow, despite supposedly progressive times, raising children remains "women's work." We're talking good cop, bad cop here, and a lot of dads never join the force.

I thought about the other talks I had given. A smattering of dads, at best. In my practice, moms accompany their teens and tweens to sessions well over ninety percent of the time. Now today, more mothers than ever work outside the home, full-time and part-time. The income gap between genders is, ever so slowly, narrowing.

It's time for a narrowing of the parenting gap.

This is a call to action for fathers. This available parenting thing is not just for moms. Your children need their fathers. And coaching a team here and there and serving as a good provider will no longer suffice. Your kids need to know that you are fully and emotionally available to them. Your role is critical. You need to be there to teach your daughters not to settle in their relationships. You need to be there to teach your sons how to treat people. You are a role model, and your children are watching. If you're unavailable, they see that as well. So come on, guys. We are made for this parenting thing. It's the most important thing we will ever do in this life.

Let's step it up!

And if you are a mom reading this book, be sure to hand it to dad when you are done.

WHY WAITING NEVER WORKS
. . . .

> "I feel like I've blown it. I'm afraid it's too
> late to get through to her."
> **—MOTHER OF REBECCA, 17**

These are busy times, and we have priorities nagging at us from all directions. I can easily see how you may be inclined to shelve this book, maybe this whole availability thing. You may feel you have time. You'll get to it, just not right now. Well, acting now is important, especially if your child is not yet a teenager.

For those of you with younger children, you have a unique opportunity, *right now*, to begin to open up communication and sustain it through adolescence.

Ah, middle school. I remember those days. In sixth, seventh, even eighth grade, a lot of us were still very much children. Young, innocent, naïve, silly. No smoking yet, certainly no drinking or drugs. I remember my friend Al kissed a girl in the stairwell in seventh grade. And that was about it for sex.

Middle school has, well, changed.

These days, it is here, in that tween-age transition from grammar school to middle school, that some of the challenges of parenting adolescents first arise. If your child is a middle-schooler, I consider you lucky to be reading this book now. Don't wait. Begin available parenting now and set the foundation for your relationship, your connection, and expectations, early.

The point is, you do not need to wait until your child is a teenager, or near teenaged, to be an available parent. Ideally, you are available early in your child's life. This way, foundations of love, trust, communication, competence and boundaries are clear long before age 13.

With your preteen, you can set your expectations early about school, homework, curfew, and other freedoms. Once they cross the line into adolescence, setting rules and boundaries becomes much tougher.

These days, believe it or not, the initial exposure to drugs, alcohol, and smoking typically takes place during the preteen years, and many children experience difficulties with self-esteem for the first time, driven by social and academic pressures and concerns. For some younger teens, sexuality begins to take center stage as well.

Remember, you are the available parent. You have a strong foundation based on a history of talking, encouraging, having a good time together, and so on. You don't have to wait for an issue to arise to bring up tough topics with your child. You don't need to hear rumors about kids coupling up or catch wind of smoking or drinking in their grade. No, you are ready to have those talks anytime. You let your child know that he will undoubtedly be confronted with these challenges. You talk to him about what he's been exposed to so far, and you *really listen*. You let your child know your expectations, and that you are available to talk about this stuff, yes, including the awkward sex stuff, anytime.

You have no fear about the power of suggestion. That is, by bringing up the tough topics of sex, drugs, or cigarettes, by entertaining the discussion with your child, you know you are not condoning the behavior. Rather, you are intelligent and curious enough to understand the realities your child faces, and you want to ensure that she is prepared ahead of time. You do not want her to be blindsided by peer pressure. You want her to be calm, clear, and intentional in her decision making, and you recognize that your best contribution is listening and talking, openly and honestly. You keep the flow of communication open, and you are as willing to listen as to speak.

You are also careful not to "pile on," trying to assuage your anxiety by addressing all the tough topics at the same time. You recognize that your young teen only has so much energy for these conversations and is only able to take so much in at once. So you space these talks out.

Believe me, your child has thoughts, concerns, worries, and fears about these topics. Not many set out to entrap themselves in maladaptive behavior. More often than not, kids take up such behaviors in order to fit in or, more accurately, for fear of *not* fitting in with peers. And peers exert an awful lot of power when it comes to these issues. But the available parent exerts more. Despite the way things may appear sometimes, you have not lost your capacity to influence your child's decision making. Good to know, right?

Parents often tell me that they notice emotional changes in their middle-schoolers, sometimes profound changes such as a more grim outlook on the world or their lives, or overt depression. Sometimes the changes are more subtle. Either way, they are a cue for you to approach your child and talk to him about what's going on, what's changing in his life. Let him know that you notice. Ask him how things are—at school, with friends. Be prepared that you may hear that your child is in more distress than you thought. More often than not, the best medicine for such matters is a caring, listening, nonjudgmental parent. He may not need a solution, just an ear. Be prepared for both. Too often, this is when parents hit the panic button and call in guys like me. These are important moments in development. Unless therapy is truly indicated, I would far prefer *you* spend these moments with your child.

By the way, I have found that the best way for a parent, or a therapist, for that matter, to begin one of these conversations is simply by asking, "How can I help?" I'm not sure exactly what it is about this question that seems to work so well with our kids. I think it gives them the feeling they are not alone in whatever decision they're confronting. Maybe it simply feels good to know that somebody understands and cares enough to participate in their lives when they're experiencing a challenge. Either way, I have found "How can I help?" to be a useful opening in relationships, particularly parent–teen relationships.

Finally, keep in mind that you have a great opportunity in the middle school years to lay a foundation of honesty, openness, and caring that will prove beneficial in the coming teen years. Open the door to availability now, and it will be much easier to keep it open later.

For those of you who already have adolescent children, your job is a bit tougher. You are charged with opening a door that may already feel closed, partly or fully. That is not to say that you are sunk if your child is already a teenager and freezing you out. It's *never* too late, but the earlier, the better.

PART THREE

WHAT ALWAYS WORKS

"My mom's fun, she's cool. She thinks I'm
da bomb. So I am."

—ELLEN, 15

CHECK YOUR EGO

"They're clueless. They don't get me, and
they don't want to. They clearly will not
settle for anything but what they want to
hear. So I give it to them. I basically have
two worlds, my reality with my friends, and
the face I show them, totally fake. Maybe it
makes them happy, I don't know."

—JAKE, 16

Think about the day when your teenager was born, the unconditional love you felt for him that day, and in the weeks, months,

and years since. Do you still feel that way today? When did that feeling change?

There is something about your child, some indelible set of personality qualities that make up who she is. She may be exceptionally talented, maybe obstinate and stubborn. Perhaps she is social, or funny, or shy. She is probably defiant, willful, and experimental.

Today, she is certainly not the person you envisioned when you first held her, not exactly who you intended her to be, who you thought you raised her to be. And, if you stop for a moment, place your ego squarely in check, and think about it, thank God for that! After all, our children are not created in *our* image—that thought is simply a manifestation of our ego at work.

Rather, your child is an entity, a personality, a person, unto herself. Most of us believe our children, all of our children, are made in *God's* image, whoever or whatever you may envision God to be. Just as we were. Just as everybody is. As parents, we're lucky. We get to borrow them for a time, to teach them, guide them, challenge them, learn from them, and perhaps most importantly, to love them unconditionally. Here is the toughest thing for many parents to hear: our children are perfect as they are. Here. Now. Exactly the way they are. So perhaps the most important question we need to ask ourselves is: Are my expressions of love for my child truly unconditional?

When a parent's love feels conditional, it can be so painfully obvious. I worked with parents of adolescents in two separate sessions one day a while back. Early in each of the conversations, it became apparent to me that they were attempting to fulfill their own needs through their adolescent children.

In the first session, it was rapidly apparent to me that Mom was invested in keeping her child "sick." At various points in the hour,

Mom diagnosed this poor girl as depressed, "manic," ADHD and just plain "nuts." I soon realized that having a sick child made her feel needed in this world. What role would she play, whom would she fix, if nothing was wrong with her daughter?

In another session, a father said he was perpetually, chronically distraught about the state of his son's life. Why isn't he involved in extracurricular activities? Why doesn't he choose to work harder in school? Why the hell does he play those damn video games all night? What kind of a kid dresses like this? Toward the end of the hour, he wondered aloud whether he was asking too much of his kid. The answer, of course, is yes.

We raise our kids to share our values. We want to raise good people, people who will become responsible adults. But there is not one absolute template for goodness, for living with values. Too often, we parents create, early in our children's lives, an ideal in our minds for how we envision them to be: what they'll wear, what they'll do, how they'll talk with other adults, and so on. What we do not take into consideration when we do this is that our children are people, not puppets.

So, as much as you may think otherwise, you do not *need* him to play football, quit smoking pot, turn down that music, do some goddamn homework, or clean that dump of a room before he is acceptable, before he is okay. He is *himself*, who he is intended to be, who he in fact *needs* to be right here, right now. When you catch him burning through a fourth straight hour texting friends about some fleeting issue you find entirely inane, keep in mind that this is playing out exactly as it needs to. Even as dishes pile up in the sink.

I know, I know. The idea is to *change* them, isn't it? We're supposed to make them better people. No, our job is to be available, to guide them, to counsel them, and then to get out of the

73

way to let them establish who they are, and let them be themselves.

I encourage you to take a deep breath here before reading on. Now, if you can look at your child, really look at him, without judgment, anger, or a need for him to be anything other than who he is, I think you will find some interesting thoughts entering your mind. You might allow yourself to remember what it is you have always loved about him. You also might be struck by all the time and energy you have been expending, perhaps over the course of years, attempting to push him in directions that clash with his true spirit. You may realize that you no longer really know much about this sweet, remarkable, perfect person you welcomed into the world not so long ago with such unadulterated joy. Is it not true, regardless of how he dresses, what he does past midnight, who he talks to online, how little he does to plan for the future, that you do not know him or appreciate him the way you'd like to?

Many of us wonder why our kids don't try, why they don't listen, why they're so unmotivated and apparently depressed, and why they're not "successful." A lot of the answers depend on the meaning of success, and who is entitled to define it. You have the option of pushing *your* meaning down your child's throat. I cannot stop you from doing that. I can tell you that, at some point, if you don't listen to what he wants in his world, there is a strong likelihood that he will eventually choose not to listen to what you want him to have in his world. How long would it take for you to stop listening to someone who did not listen to you?

You the parent, I believe, are the primary key to the success of your child. In my work, I have witnessed time and time and time again parents who dismiss and effectively disown their adolescent children because they do not agree with some of their choices. Please keep in mind that this is *your* ego at work, not your child's. Once you judge, once you dismiss, once you reject, once you close off communication and become unavailable, you stack the deck higher and higher against the success not only of your relationship, but of your child as well. I intend that statement to be less a scare tactic and more a call to arms. My point is that you *always* have the power, through insight and self-awareness, to change this dynamic in your relationship. And you can do so without losing your authority to parent your teen. Once your ego is out of the way of your parenting, you can begin to listen to your intuition, and trust your instincts with your children. With your ego in the way, your inner voice is clouded by your own perceived needs, and it is far less useful to you in making decisions.

For a moment, picture yourself at your child's age. How would you describe the teen that you were? How would your parents have described you? How did things turn out for you? Really? By and large, pretty well? So what makes you think your child's adolescence will bring your world, their world, or your collective world to an end?

Don't Make It about You

> "My dad makes me feel like just another
> chapter in his book."
>
> —MASON, 16

You know you are still operating from ego-based thinking when you catch yourself saying "Look what her behavior is doing to me!" An alarming number of teenagers have also complained to me about another ego-driven parenting phenomenon. As one teenage client of mine so simply and eloquently stated, "Take care of your kids, man. Don't make your kids take care of you."

John happens to be a football player. An acclaimed running back at his high school, John made the varsity squad in his sophomore year. The local newspaper projects he will be a strong prospect to play Division I ball, and he has already been contacted by a few college scouts. Imagine my surprise when he came to my office recently and announced he will probably not continue to play football in his upcoming junior season.

> *"Well, why wouldn't you play, John? You're a superstar, and the team is supposed to be a contender this year for the State Championship."*
>
> *"Yeah, I know. It's just that I never really wanted this in the first place."*
>
> *"But you've worked so hard and come so far. Why would you do so if you never really wanted it?"*

John went on to explain that he never really enjoyed playing football all that much. As it turns out, what John has really been seeking, ever since he first put on pads and a helmet and laced up spikes in the fifth grade, was his father's attention and approval. John's father was a well-known college football player in his day. Even now, he lives, eats, and breathes the sport. As a matter of fact, the few times he joined John and me for sessions, he was always sporting football gear: a Notre Dame jersey, a Michigan cap, or an Ohio State sweatshirt.

Now, his father attended every game, every single game, John ever played. He coached John during grammar school and continued "coaching" him, play by play, for hours after games through this past season. John said it was as if he carried game film around in his head.

> *"See, you gotta get around that corner a little sooner, buddy, to get those extra couple yards."*
> *"Use the stiff-arm I taught you if a guy ever comes after you like that again."*

And then there was John's favorite, his father pleading, *"Hands, John! Use those hands!"* As if he was *trying* to drop the pass!

Though his father was often critical, John admitted to me that he craved his attention and approval. He worked hard to follow his father's advice, which John agrees was always excellent.

John also fondly recalled memories from his younger years: crisp, endless autumn weekends when he would sit in his father's lap and they would watch football together. His father would point out to him why a play worked or failed, the finer points of different offensive plays, and, of course, why the Packers suck every year, regardless of their record. After games, they would go out in the yard and play together, father and son, QB and running back, creating perfect reenactments of the afternoon's touchdowns. John beams as he reflects on those animated times with his father.

Outside of football, however, John described life with his father as effectively nonexistent, aside from the fact that the two of them resided under the same roof. They exchanged few words in the course of an ordinary day, and those words rarely carried any weight or import. His father would approach the closed bedroom door, knock lightly, and ask if John had finished his homework, eaten supper, or let the dog out. He'd offer momentary lectures on responsibility.

John laughed as he told me this, saying that his father's delivery was so wooden that he sounded as if he was reading from an old parenting manual from the fifties! Sadly, even these few exchanges did not feel sincere to John. John would answer the mundane question, and his dad would disappear down the hallway.

Still, John felt that, if nothing else, he would always have football as a special thing between his dad and himself. From the Kickoff Classic in late August to the Super Bowl the following February, John's father watched football all weekend and anytime there was a game on cable during the week. Unfortunately, as John got older, even the football experience changed with his father. John described an instance recently when his father was watching a Chicago Bears game. John sat down on the couch to join him, hoping they could connect and talk about the game, but his father was so engrossed that he hushed John rudely every time he spoke. John painfully described his dad's posture, leaning forward toward the television, focusing so much on the game, as if John himself was not even in the room. Season after season, John says he sits down in that room, hoping to connect with his dad, only to feel him slipping further away. John joked morosely that the Bears lost the Super Bowl the same season he lost his dad.

"I play football to stay connected to my dad, to tell you the truth. I really don't care about it, but *he* does, so at least we have something, right? I like the conversations after the games all right, I guess. It's the only time he seems to know what to do with me. Basically, I just feel like it is my job to take care of him and make conversation, and not the other way around."

His father's interest, in the end, turned out to be the only reason John stayed connected to football. It was his way of taking care of his father, of managing his father's job of connection. Imagine the heartbreak of the available child of an unavailable parent.

John felt the burden of the lack of connection with his father every day, and the lion's share of his behavior was an attempt to foster and deepen that connection, a connection his father treated in so cavalier a manner. John was forever hurt by his father, but never felt he could say so. After all, his father was a manly man, a football guy. John wondered how he would feel about having a son who was so soft as to care about relationships.

Now, take a moment and consider all that John's father is missing out on in his life and the life of his son. Despite his own uncaring behavior, his teenage son continues to love him and crave his attention. His son is loyal, honest, sensitive, and loving. But this man makes a choice, every day, to be blind to his son's true presence in his life. And time passes, along with opportunity, hope, and, one can assume, a child's love. A heartbreaking, true story. And to think, with just a little availability and a little less ego on the part of this man, a very different story would emerge. I am very fond of John, and I hope that one day, before it is too late, his father shares this sense of fondness and opens himself up to become an available parent.

John has sound advice for parents: Take care of your teenager. Take the responsibility of fostering a connection with him. Don't require him to reach out to you, to take care of you. It's not a fair thing to ask of a teen, and he's not emotionally equipped for the task.

So what, specifically, can John's father do to change things? Good question. First, he can show a genuine interest in John's world by *asking* instead of *telling*. He might ask John about his interests. He might ask how he feels about football these days. He might ask what's going on at school and with his friends. He can be open to hearing what John has to say, even if it does not reflect perfectly what he wants to hear. John's dad proved to be a good coach, but not a great listener. The best way to get to know your teen is to ask and listen, a lot. And please, don't get me wrong about John's dad. I believe he is a loving father who cares deeply for his son. His son, however, rarely feels this love. To John, his father's love feels conditional: he's good enough as long as he's playing football and playing well. His father can change this dynamic with a few open, loving, listening interactions.

It's all a matter of availability.

The Wish List

At this point, I would like you to participate in a simple but powerful exercise. Find a nice, quiet place in your home where you can sit with pen and paper. Now take a moment and write a wish list for your teenager. Write down what you want for him socially, emotionally, academically, athletically, musically, and in any other pertinent areas of his life, now and in the future. Write down one or two wishes in each category. Do not read on until you complete your list. And no cheating!

In parenting workshops, coaching, and my clinical work, I often ask parents to concoct such a list. After administering this exercise a number of times, I have found that a certain theme emerges. We need to be aware of when our wishes for our kids are driven by our own ego. An example of an ego-driven response would be "I would like Robert to get straight A's through high school so that he can continue the family tradition of attending Harvard." An example of a more ego-free response might be "I would like Jack to get good grades so that he feels competent and his options remain open" or "I would like Bethany to experience closeness, trust, and fulfillment in her peer relationships, setting a foundation for positive, loving relationships in the future."

I would like you to review your list honestly and evaluate the nature of each of your wishes. I have found this to be an important exercise, as it tends to uncover, in a slightly sneaky manner I'll admit, that which drives an awful lot of our parenting behavior. I do not expect any parent to be perfect here, by the way. I think we all harbor wishes, be they secret or overt, regarding the unfolding lives of our teens. If your wish for your teen is ego-driven, however, it is far less likely to reflect *her* dreams and desires and will likely lead to rifts and complications in your relationship. Oh, and it probably won't come true either. A wish driven by openness and availability, on the other hand, is likely to foster competence, connection, and understanding between you and your teen. I don't think I need to ask which dynamic you find more appealing or successful.

Keep this exercise in mind as you continue to work through this book. Once you have read it through, I encourage you to repeat the exercise. In my experience, your wishes will increasingly reflect availability.

EMOTIONAL ROLE-MODELING: FORGIVE ME, FATHER

Often, taking care of your teen means taking care of yourself first. As a parent, you need to know and understand your own emotional life well in order to model emotional management for your teenager. Just telling your teenager to "get himself under control" does not suffice. You need to exhibit and model self-control and emotional self-awareness.

A client of mine, Hank, revealed recently that he has trouble regulating and monitoring his emotions when in conflict with his teenage son. He told me of a recent episode in which his son was laughing and horsing around with his siblings at church, writing down funny phrases and passing them back and forth. Hank lost it, scolding his son, red-faced, mid-sermon. He admitted to yelling, through clenched teeth, "This is not the way we behave in church, godammit!" Immediately, there was silence. Everywhere. Hank knew this was not good. To hear him tell it, he slowly lifted his gaze to see a congregation in still life, each pair of eyes staring straight at him, mouths agape in unison. At the pulpit, the pastor mirrored the crowd's stunned response.

In retrospect, Hank was mortified at his *own* behavior. Not until he analyzed his feelings in session did he realize that his anger involved control issues between himself and his own father, and his corresponding fears and feelings of incompetence as a father himself. Hank realized he was laying all of this emotional weight on his son, who was of course ill-equipped to manage it. Fortunately, after talking it through, Hank is far more aware of the thoughts and emotions that drive his own behavior. As a result, he has learned to minimize conflict with his son and manage it far better and more coolly when it does arise. He can now serve as a role model of emotional self-regulation for his son, instead of teaching him how to creatively lose it through clenched teeth in the middle of a sermon.

Sometimes this dynamic can be significantly more damaging than in Hank's case. I know a father whose moods are wildly unpredictable to his teenage daughter. She never knows whether he'll be sweet or blind with fury, and it is obvious she does not know what to do in his presence. "What can I do that won't piss him off?" she asks. She is increasingly unsure of herself around him and in most social situations, and her sense of security is as affected as her fragile self-esteem. This can be one of the most harmful family dynamics, and it happens a lot. Further, I have noted that the other parent is often willing to look the other way to preserve the peace. This, my friends, is bullshit. Peace is never preserved with this dynamic at play; the unrest sits in the pit of your child's stomach—absolutely unacceptable. Lack of emotional regulation on the part of a parent is the polar opposite of availability. So, if this dynamic plays out in your family, you need to do something to change it, right away.

If you frequently find yourself responding to your teen through impulse and anger, I strongly encourage you to investigate the source of your feelings. Often, it has little to do with your teenager, and as a result she is unsure how to respond when you react in an overly emotional manner. You probably detect a disturbing breakdown in communication when this takes place.

Undoing this type of communication problem can be tricky. You may find it easy to attribute an emotional outbreak on your part simply to the difficulty of raising a teenager. I suggest you consider the arc of your life story, as Hank so wisely chose to do, in order to identify the emotional source of your feelings. If you have significant difficulty identifying the issues embedded in your relationship with your teen, I suggest you seek the help of a qualified psychologist to help you sort it out. This may be the most important step you can take toward availability in your relationship with your teenager.

TAPPING YOUR INTUITION

Our lives are so very crowded and busy. We work. We drive. We look at the clock. We worry. We spend. We cook. We clean. We push. We step aside. We try to remain calm. We yell. We go to bed. We work. We get lost sometimes in this material world. Even those of us who protect the time for religious services often struggle with remaining fully present in that seat, kneeler, or pew. There is so much demand to think of all that needs to be done once the final prayer is recited. Worry about the future too often robs us of the precious present.

It is holding on to and remaining in the present, though, that allows us to channel our inner voice, our intuition and availability, to really hear ourselves and discover who we are. For most parents, this sense of self should be primary among the goals we have for our children, especially as they become teenagers. In order to model this process for them, however, we need to be able to hear ourselves, to get in touch with our own core intuitive sense, our availability. We need to learn to be in—and stay in—the here and now, and recognize that which is truly important.

Once you recognize the part of you that is ego-driven and you jettison that element from your repertoire, you will have uncovered something amazing within yourself as a parent. You will find that you have a far clearer sense of intuition. Ego draws you away from your presence of mind, clouding and distorting intuition, such that you cannot fully trust your thoughts and decision making. As you become more in touch with your intuition, I would encourage you to follow it entirely in your available parenting. You won't need to rely on the thoughts and opinions of other parents or friends, or even the advice offered in this book. You will know, intuitively, the right approach to your teen.

GAINING TRACTION

> "Don't make every issue an 'us versus you' thing. What parents don't know is that, mostly, their kids want to like them. If the whole friggin' house is at war, though, forget it. Nobody's happy. Not good times."
>
> —CHRISTOPHER, 16

DEPOSITS IN THE EMOTIONAL BANK ACCOUNT

You may be thinking that you are doing everything right in making yourself available to your teenager, and yet something is still not working. You don't feel connected to her, or she doesn't seem to listen to you. You're probably wondering why you've got so little traction in your relationship, why your words are so readily dismissed. A brilliant little concept from the literature on Emotional Intelligence comes in handy here: the Emotional Bank Account.

By way of example, let me tell you about two partners in an accounting firm, their plush offices side by side. I worked as an auditor for this firm (a long story for a different book) and was assigned to projects under the watchful eyes of each of these men. The first partner, we'll call him Bill, was perhaps the most brilliant financial mind I have ever encountered. From basic debits and credits to balance sheets and income statements, Bill was the guy who knew all the answers or could easily figure them out. I should also mention here that Bill was frightfully, wretchedly *mean*. Like tear-your-head-off-in-front-of-everybody-in-the-staff-room mean. Bill knew the answers, but we were all deathly afraid to ask the questions. To be called into his office was a terrifying experience, as you knew you were about to be royally chewed out, regardless of the nature of the transgression. He was not into listening, just productivity. He had a way of making everyone around him feel less competent, and the MO of the majority of the staff was to avoid Bill at all costs. Even Bill's clients were afraid of him; I heard him screech at more than one of them for their incompetence in preparing the financial documents we needed to get our work done.

In the office next to Bill was Greg, a sweet, laid-back guy with a slight Southern drawl and a very good sense of humor. Greg may very well have been an accounting whiz, but I can't say I know for sure. His style was to let his staff describe the work to the client, while he sat back, listening and nodding. In a typical client meeting, Greg would simply ask the client, "So, how does this sit with you? Anything we can do to make it work better for you?" The inevitable result in a Greg meeting was that the client would leave laughing and fully satisfied that they were being taken care of.

I remember one afternoon when Greg came into our bullpen of a staff room to talk to me. He asked about my girlfriend and my recent trip to Los Angeles. We spent quite a bit of time talking about his son's struggles in soccer. We joked around a little bit. That was it. Nothing about work, no assignments. Just a chat. This was Greg's way.

Now, being a keen observer of human behavior, I began to notice that people, myself included, seemed to like working for Greg a lot more than Bill. They were willing to work longer hours when asked, with far fewer gripes. The reason is that Greg understood the concept of the Emotional Bank Account, and he always kept a nice balance in the accounts with all of his clients and staff.

By way of definition, the Emotional Bank Account is the emotional result of the quality of time spent in a relationship. A positive balance in the account provides a strong foundation for a relationship, any relationship, such that the relationship thrives and grows whenever things are going well, and is also resilient through more difficult times. A negative balance tends to breed a combination of hostility and avoidance. A zero balance can foster a sense of ambivalence and insecurity. Strangely enough, there is an actual accounting term that matches up nicely with a balance in the Emotional Bank Account. It is, of course, an asset, appropriately named *goodwill*.

I love this concept. I have found the Emotional Bank Account useful in just about every relationship in every area of my life, from my personal life to my clinical work to my workshops and talks for businesses, couples, and of course, parents. You may be wondering how this applies to your relationship with your teenager. Well, this relationship has Emotional Bank Accounts as well. Quite simply, if you don't carry a positive balance of goodwill in that account, it is unreasonable to expect your teenager to respond to you in a positive way. Herein lies the reason that so many teens seem to blow off their parents. They believe you will be more of a Bill than a Greg. That's the bad news.

Now here's the good news. The Emotional Bank Account is always open for deposits. What does this mean? Effectively, it means that if you have a relationship with your teen that feels disconnected and distant, you have the power to change this circumstance, anytime. By adding some goodwill, you have the power to influence your teen in a genuine, positive way, and she will become increasingly invested in your relationship and your point of view. Without a positive balance, you become frustrated that all your well-intended parental interventions seem to fall away ineffectually. Eventually, with no positive balance, your influence consists primarily of punishment—withholding of allowance, negotiations about curfew and the use of the car, and so on. These punishments do not hold nearly the same influential value in parent–teen relationships as in the Emotional Bank Account. You'll find them to be far less effective than you might think. And they are no fun.

In your relationship with your teenager, goodwill might consist of encouraging words before a test. It might mean sitting down and talking about a difficult social situation, without offering quick suggestions or judgments. It might mean simply telling your child you love him. It might mean acknowledging his feelings during a stressful time. Perhaps you just let him know you're available should he ever want to talk, without insisting that he talk. Regardless of what you choose as deposits, it is critical that your gestures be genuine. Teenagers are expert at picking up on the disingenuous show of love. You don't have to be perfect and choreographed, but he will know if you are not being yourself.

Let me use my own father as an example. For as far back as I can remember, every day that I saw him through childhood and adolescence until the day he died, my father kissed me on the forehead (standing on his toes by the time I was 16) and told me he loved me. He never once played catch with me when I was a kid. We did not have long, involved talks about the meaning of life. There were a lot of things he could have done differently. But this gesture, this kiss, meant everything to me. With each kiss, I knew he loved me unconditionally. I knew he supported me, and I knew he believed I was special. To my thinking, Walt Duffy's forehead kisses will always be the ultimate deposit in the Emotional Bank Account, sufficient for me to look up to him and heed his words.

Now, let's spend some time discussing ways in which you can gain the traction you need in your relationship. As we continue the discussion on available parenting, keep the Emotional Bank Account in mind.

Simple Acknowledgment

It's amazing what can happen when you recognize and acknowledge some special quality in a teen. It can reap benefits well beyond a growing balance in the Emotional Bank Account. I began working with Nathan during his sophomore year. To me, he seemed the classic slacker. He smoked pot. He was a skateboarder. He hated school. He was exceptionally laid back, referring to me as "Dude" from the first session. He would stretch out on my couch to the point where I thought he might as well just lie down and take a nap. He was a one-word-answer guy. In our early sessions together, I know I worked a lot harder than he did. I made assumptions about Nathan. I thought he was limited in what he would be able to accomplish. He kept coming for therapy, because, in his words, "You're a righteous-enough dude. And it gets me out of doing other stuff my 'rents want me to do. Peace!"

After a while, I felt we were stagnating in our work, but Nathan probably would have kept coming endlessly. One day, Nathan came in to tell me that a boy in his grade had just passed away from juvenile diabetes. He struggled trying to describe his feelings, choking back tears. He told me he felt weird being affected by the death, indicating that this boy was more an acquaintance than a close friend. But he admitted he was greatly affected nonetheless. I thanked Nathan for his emotional honesty, and I shared that I saw in him a depth, maturity, and sense of empathy I had never witnessed before. For the first time ever in my presence, Nathan sat up straight. He looked me in the eye. He told other stories. He started *working*. Never before had I seen a more instantaneous change in a client.

The change in Nathan since that day been almost incomprehensible to me. He has continued to work both in and out of sessions. He started making headway in school. He even combed his hair!

One day, he came in and told me about a major project he had to do for school. He said that he had planned on faking his way through with something half-assed, as he did with so much of his schoolwork before. Instead, he decided to do something truly extraordinary. He organized and ran a fund-raising event for juvenile diabetes research. He found a venue, booked bands, made phone calls and fliers. I was so proud of him. More importantly, Nathan felt good about himself. He found his way.

He still calls me "Dude," but there is clarity in Nathan's eye now, a determination in his voice, a backbone and conviction that were not there before. I know the loss had something to do with the change. I also know, in my heart, that feeling understood, acknowledged, and appreciated as something other than a slacker affected Nathan deeply as well. Recognition and acknowledgment can certainly help increase the balance in the Emotional Bank Account, and as Nathan's story shows, it can also alter the course of a teen's life.

THE MULTIPLE BENEFITS OF LAUGHTER

> "I got home kinda late, and my dad starts yelling at me, and he spits on himself. We both started cracking up! It was awesome!"
>
> —DAVID, 17

They say we're not supposed to be friends with our kids, that part of the problem with families today is we're trying to be our kid's best pal instead of his parent. What he needs in a parent, they say, is someone who will provide guidance, structure, and discipline.

It seems we're beginning to think that if we enjoy our relationship with our child, if we have fun talking with him, then somehow we are coming up short as parents. Well, I don't think so. I think it is important, perhaps critical, that we enjoy our children, that we play with them and celebrate with them. If we lack this connection, I think we also lack the "juice" to have influence in their lives as well, to provide guidance, structure, and discipline. This would be a significant loss all around.

It's not the only loss we would experience. I read recently that children laugh an average of 185 times a day. Adults, 15 times. Somewhere along the line, we lose our ability to laugh at life, at ourselves, at *anything*. I think that as we grow older and wiser (?), we lose something very important, our sensibility toward laughter. Sadly, I think we ritually replace our laughter with fear. I think we should learn to take a page from our children's book and learn to laugh again. I can say that this is a gift my son returned to me, but only because I was willing to accept it. Now, he's funny as hell, so he gave me little choice. I now laugh all the time, again. Laughter requires us to strip away, at least some of the time, the veneer of adulthood. It allows us to be goofy, sardonic, ridiculous. Sometimes it even requires us to poke fun at ourselves. Laughter brings instant perspective.

Laughter also contributes greatly to the richness of your relationship with your child. If you can laugh with your child during the smooth times, your relationship will be all the more resilient during the rough times. Laugh during the tough times—you'll find connections and solutions come so much easier. Believe me, laughter brightens even the darkest of days. Note that if you're going to instill levity and humor in your relationship, it has to be genuine, based on your experiences together. Nothing is more off-putting to a teenager than forced, contrived attempts at humor. This is an important point, because a disingenuous gesture can drive a wedge between you and simply reinforce your "You're a dork, you don't get me" reputation. I see this *all* the time. Forced, artificial, programmed humor and fun are the antithesis of availability.

And you don't have to be Seinfeld to connect with humor. Instead, just be genuine, and be prepared to laugh, even at yourself. Pay attention to what your child finds funny—with you, their siblings, and their friends. Pay attention to what he watches on TV. Or just listen for his laughter and pay attention. And don't be afraid to dig deep into the family archives. Tell your own stories, and not only those where you end up the hero. Recall for them those times when you laughed hardest. They may just see you in a different light than ever before. Children also love to hear stories of what they were like when they were younger, especially the mishaps and missteps. I have seen years of disconnect drain away with a story of a Christmas gone wrong years ago or a ruined vacation moment. I can recall one family, in significant crisis, mind you, cracking up to the point of tears recalling stories of a wedding nearly a decade earlier—the bad clothes, the drunken uncle, the lousy band. With that, they were back in business: reconnected.

THE OZZY CONNECTION:
STEP OUTSIDE YOUR COMFORT ZONE

Friends of mine, parents of a 13-year-old boy named Thomas, offered me a bizarre, most excellent story about the Emotional Bank Account and the parent–teen connection. Thomas came to them and said he wanted to attend a concert, an Ozzy Osbourne concert. Mom and Dad's initial impulse was an obvious one. After all, wasn't Ozzy the guy who bit the head off a live bat during one of his shows? Or was it a dove? Either way, he bit the head off something, something live, and this hardly seemed like the wholesome fare they pictured for their sweet 13-year-old boy. The truth is, though, that Thomas was a huge Ozzy fan, whether Mom and Dad liked it or not.

So, instead of simply shutting him out, Mom and Dad kicked off a process of negotiations with Thomas. Should you be allowed to attend this, this *concert*, how will you and your friends get there? Who will pay for the tickets? After much negotiation and soul-searching, they decided they wanted Thomas to have the experience of attending, despite the fact that it clearly would not be the experience they would have chosen for him. They further decided that, for safety reasons, Thomas and friends needed to be accompanied by adults. Mom drew the short straw.

And so it was that two preppy, buttoned-down moms accompanied four young teenage boys 40 miles from home to witness their very first Ozzfest. Of course, first and foremost, the moms had to decide what they themselves would wear. They knew they would be atypical audience members going in, but they did not want to stick out too much. So for one bizarre summer night, they relegated the cable-knit sweaters and khakis to the back of the closet in favor of basic T-shirts and jeans. One can only guess that to complete the look, they dragged out of mothballs some long-abandoned rock-and-roll attitude for the festivities.

Well, Thomas's mom reports to me that she actually had a good time. First, she allowed Thomas his first concert experience. By attending, she also pushed the envelope a bit for herself, a little adventure for both mother and son. Rock on, Mom.

There's a story about this experience that I just love. During ovations between songs, as one might guess, Ozzy yelled out a number of times, "I can't fuckin' hear ya." On the way home, Mom and her son joked in the car:

"Wasn't Ozzy awesome, Mom?"

Mom, with her best slurred British accent: *"Sorry 'Omas. Can't fu'in' hear ya!"*

This line comes up sometimes at home even now, and the whole family just laughs. Now, Mom could easily have gone the route of lecturing about the appropriate use of language and what she and Dad approve of and disapprove of, and so on. But she recognized that her son knows all that, so she picked a different route. Hilarity and connection ensued. A little levity trumps a lecture any day, don't you think?

These parents had this advice for parents of teens everywhere: "When they come to you, relax your trigger finger. Don't just say 'no.' Listen and let them tell you about it and make a proposal. You might be surprised at the ideas and compromises you can arrive at together. When you do this, it all works out in the end. And even if you don't enjoy the experience, it too shall pass."

They know "it too shall pass" because of Thomas's ever-shifting interests. Before it was Ozzy, it was the WWF, then NASCAR, then skateboarding. Never once did these parents say they regretted supporting Thomas instead of shutting him down. Staying connected to him and sustaining a healthy balance in the Emotional Bank Account were more important to them than whether they were interested in attending some event. For them, there is really no comparison.

These are inspiring, available parents.

COMMUNICATION AND CONNECTION

> "My parents are all about grades, nothing else. I feel like my mom has something against me all the time. She snoops, looking for things I've done wrong. It scares me. A lot. Like she's looking for a reason to send me away or something. If I thought she really cared, I'd talk to her. Parents should be clear that they care about their kids, and that they're not going to be a big threat to them."
>
> —REBECCA, 14

Does your adolescent seem to like you? Do you get one-word answers to every question? Is he willing to spend *some* time with you? If he avoids you just about all the time, you definitely have an issue on your hands. The good news is that this trouble can be circumvented. But without communication, without talking, we've got nothing.

Effective communication is, of course, critical to availability. I find that, more often than not, parents try to overtalk with their teens about what they're doing wrong—the painfully ineffective lectures. I encourage you to sharply limit this type of communication. Not only is it ineffective, but it also damages your credibility with your teen. Believe me, I know this from experience.

You know how insidious maladaptive patterns of communication can become in families. Patterns of poor communication, of miscommunication, of denial and repression, too often trickle from one generation to the next as easily as autumn leaves drifting down family trees. If you are like, well, *everybody*, your family probably contains one or more of these destructive patterns. As your child becomes a teenager, you have a unique opportunity to break negative communication cycles that may go back decades, some of them even centuries. Think about how powerful a positive change you can exert here. Imagine the growing balance in the Emotional Bank Account.

I grew up in what I would describe as a rather repressive home. During the early years of my childhood, we were, by many accounts, a "perfect" family. As my older siblings reached adolescence, however, the image of my home and family began to fragment. Some of my siblings began to experience fairly profound challenges. The tightening constriction around communication became palpable in my house, and the familial message was clear: these matters stay within these walls. As difficulties escalated, we fell increasingly silent about them, to the outside world and to one another. As a result, we became an anxious, repressive, fearful household: When will the next harrowing, bad-news phone call come about my brother? When will my sister walk away and leave us? We were afraid and covertly forbade one another to talk about our fear. Those of us who were not "the issue," typically my older brother and I, suffered in a toxic, anxious silence, maintaining our "perfect" behavior to balance the household stress scales.

Over the years, I have learned that this repressive communication pattern did not start with my family and my siblings. My mother grew up an only child in a terribly quiet, judgmental, demanding household. She describes a hostile, lonely environment. When I look at photos of her as a child, it is difficult for me to imagine the poverty of emotion she suffered during those stark years. I have a strong hunch that, were my grandparents still alive, they would have similar stories to share about their own childhoods, perhaps even more harsh. And if we could conduct interviews going back generations, I'll bet there were anxious and repressive households generations ago on another continent altogether, proving that neither time nor geography are guaranteed to heal all familial wounds.

In any event, given my mother's early life, she has done a remarkable job becoming more open and available, even after suffering some tragic losses, and even as she grows older. It is never too late for availability, and it can be exceptionally healing to parent-child relationships. Due to personal work we each have done over the years, I am closer to my mother now than I have ever been. We are each more available to the other. I often wonder, though, what my childhood home would have been like with open, available communication.

AVAILABILITY VERSUS UNAVAILABILITY: THE POWER OF MUSIC

A friend of mine recently provided an illustration of the effects of available versus unavailable parents. My friend Matt has always been talented musically. He and his best friend in high school, Jason, also quite talented, formed a band together. They often collaborated on writing music and lyrics, and Matt recalls that they frequently struggled thematically with their material. There was a heavy darkness, anger, and rage in Jason's words and music that Matt simply did not relate to. In contrast, there was a lightness and optimism woven through Matt's music that seemed in retrospect to confound Jason.

Matt attributes much of the difference in their styles to the ways in which they were parented as teens. Matt's parents were highly supportive of his choice to become a musician. They listened to his music, offering praise and constructive criticism. Matt told me that he knows his music was different from the music his parents grew up with, but they recognized and accepted that styles change with each generation, so they were nonjudgmental throughout. As a result, Matt felt free to create his music, his way.

Matt describes Jason's family story quite differently. A talented musician himself, Jason rarely received recognition from his parents for his music. His father thought it was a waste of time, and his parents rarely showed up for gigs. Jason felt rejected and angry a lot of the time and sensed very little connection with his parents because he noted, correctly, that his parents simply did not "get" him. This easily solves the riddle of the bile-filled music and lyrics Jason seemed to produce so readily in high school.

During a recent jam session in Matt's basement, he and I played an old folk song called "Freight Train," and he was nice enough to play at my level, which I greatly appreciated. He told me that he learned that song originally playing with his father when he was younger, and he went on to recount fond memories of father-son jam sessions, how great a time they had, and how strong a connection he felt. In fact, Matt and his father are so close even today that Matt now works with him in the family business. In this conversation, I found myself happy not only for Matt, but also for his father and the great relationship he continues to share with his adult son. See, available parenting pays off, well past adolescence. Matt has a son of his own now, and I've got to think that this is a lucky boy who will benefit from a highly available father.

I wonder what songs they'll play together.

I love Matt's story. It really illustrates how powerful music can be in fostering a connection. But you don't have to break out guitars and banjos in order for music to change your relationship. By and large, teenagers love to *share* their music. I actually discovered this fact quite by accident. I bought a stereo for my office to listen to music between sessions. Several years ago, as

I started working with teenagers, some teen would occasionally ask if they could bring a CD or their iPod to their session for me to hear their music. Initially, being a good, by-the-book clinician, I of course refused such requests in favor of a predetermined treatment plan. So there was no music in my office during sessions for some time.

Then came young Steven. At 15, he was belligerent and uncommunicative in sessions with me. He would avoid speaking, eye contact, anything that might satisfy my clinical curiosity. This went on for several sessions. I found myself scrambling for the checkerboard, a deck of cards, the Rorschach drawings. He would have none of it. In a last-ditch attempt, out of frustration and desperation, I asked Steven if he would like to bring in music. Momentarily, he lit up.

"You mean, you would listen to what I listen to?"

"Yeah."

"In here?"

"Yeah, sure."

"There's bad words in it."

Bring it on, Steven.

And so there I sat, a therapist at work listening to Eminem for the first time. I had heard about Eminem before. A parent's worst nightmare, he apparently encouraged drugs and disobedience, loathed women, and was unforgivably vulgar. For weeks, Steven and I talked about what he liked about Eminem. Not only did this reclusive, secretive young man share with me the songs he liked, but he highlighted lyrics that, in particular, "spoke" to him. Suddenly, we were relating. Curiously, I also discovered that I really like Eminem's music, which I had written off entirely before ever having listened to it. Interesting.

Well, thanks to Steven, a whole new adolescent therapy technique was born for me, and the stereo in my office gets a lot of play. I have worked with more than one teenager who automatically plugs his iPod into the stereo, spins the wheel to Shuffle, and hits Play as a ritual to start the session. Periodically, we refer to the music, and the rest of the time it adds a nice soundtrack to the hour.

Well, bully for me, but how will this music angle help you? I hear you. It's like this. My hunch is that your teen, like Steven, is into music as well. Just as we all are—it's universal. Think back to your first Springsteen concert, or the first time your older sister put on a Stones album. Or were you more of a Madonna or Billy Joel fan? Black Sabbath? Metallica? It doesn't matter—we all come of age to our own unique soundtrack, and your teen is no different.

So, do you know what's on her iPod? If not, I encourage you to make it a regular practice to ask. And listen to it with her. Talk about it, without judging. You might find that you enjoy the music, but even if you don't, it will provide you some insight into her current mind-set. Believe me, this is parental gold. This is perhaps the number one way to get to know your kid—listen to her music, keeping your mind and your heart open.

You might want to make a game of it, in the mode of one inventive family I worked with a couple of years ago. I was seeing them as a family to resolve their relationship problems, in particular a distinct lack of communication. Well, as had become my practice by then, I suggested that the parents listen to their son's music. Dad, a music buff and historian in his own right, agreed. But he had a stipulation. The deal had to be reciprocal: For every song of yours I listen to, you need to hear one of mine. The deal was struck.

Within a few sessions, father and son were talking about music a lot, comparing and contrasting different bands and sounds. I distinctly remember them having an obvious blast arguing playfully over whether Tom Petty or the Stones could ever measure up against Nine Inch Nails or Rage Against the Machine. Over the course of the next couple of years, they went to each other's concerts together. Although the boy is off to college, they still talk frequently about bands, new albums, and who's written the better lyrics, Dylan or Cobain. Of course, it's all academic. The answers don't matter—the process does. A relationship blossomed where before there was none.

Never underestimate the power of music.

OTHER WAYS TO CONNECT

> "My best friend talks to his dad all the time because he'll come out and play street hockey and football with us. That's a cool dad."
>
> —JACOB, 15

Of course, music is not the only common ground you will be able to find with your teenager if you are willing to look and be a bit open and flexible. Sit and play his video game with him for a while. Read the same book and talk about that. Shoot some hoops with him before dinner and touch base with him on the blacktop. Adolescents are often reluctant to talk with their parents. It is an old, very effective therapist tool to engage in some activity with a child who is not forthcoming in communicating; they are far more likely to open up when they are doing something. This is true of boys in particular. If you struggle to find any other "quality" time, talk with your teen in that sequestered, protected time you inevitably spend in the car together. The idea is to protect time, even if it is just a few moments of time a day, to touch base with your teenager, let him know he matters to you, let him know you care. This is among the interventions I recommend most to parents in my practice, even when their teenager is going through some troubling times. They need to hear the good things about themselves from you, not just the bad. Just as when they were younger, they need time now to feel loved, wanted, even cherished.

One mom recently described her 16-year-old daughter as rude, immature, and just plain mean to the entire family. She would pick fights with her parents and siblings several times a day. Curiously enough, at the end of the day this daughter wanted nothing more than to cuddle with her mother for a few moments. Once we introduced (or, more likely, reintroduced), this affection into her life, this girl rapidly became more amiable and pleasant. Both Mom and daughter began to look forward to their end-of-day talks, and Mom tells me she feels as if their connection has been reestablished. It's no puzzle, really. Her daughter once again felt loved, wanted, and even cherished.

Note that this protected time is absolutely *not* the time to tell her she needs to be doing better in school or she needs to stop partying. Protect other times for those things. If you protect this "connecting" time, I think you may just find a decreasing need for the other.

MAKING THE MOST OF MOMENTS
A very available and attentive mom of three teenagers, two boys and a girl, came to see me recently. She checked in every month or two for a little parent coaching, and she was clearly stressed at the onset of this session. She indicated that there was no crisis, but she feared things were slipping between her, her husband, and their teenagers. As she described it, the problem centered around the kids' resistance to a simple, hour-long family meeting every Sunday night. She was very serious about this.

But I laughed.

I didn't mean to, but I did. Confused, she asked what my deal was, and was kind enough to stifle a comment on the obvious lack of empathy in my response.

I explained that today, I would *never* expect teenagers to be game for an hour-long meeting. And if it didn't come to pass, I certainly wouldn't see it as a failure of parenting.

We have to remember that the world our kids have grown up in varies in a very important way from our teenage world. Everything moves at warp speed now. We don't call. We text. We don't look things up. We Google. We don't wait. We go. Now.

We can debate for days about whether this pace is a good thing for our children, for society, and so on. But we cannot deny that this is their pace, the only speed they know. They didn't create it. They have just been absorbed into it.

So, with our teenagers today, rarely will we get hours. Only occasionally will we get minutes. We need to make the most of moments. This is a *moment* culture.

This is not bad news. It's just different. So, instead of hours (and did we really give our parents rapt attention for hours, really?), we have moments. But we have the opportunity for a lot of them. And they can take many forms. And they can be every bit as meaningful as hours, maybe more so.

We can text. A quick "Hi" or a "How was the Spanish test?" or a "Did you see that touchdown?" or an "I love you" can go an awfully long way. Maybe a funny picture. Or video. We can call, and just say "Hey." We can "friend." A quick hug before school. We have options.

Whatever your method, I strongly encourage you to make the most of the moments. Don't spend too much time lamenting the hours. Take them if and when you get them. But take those moments. With little effort, they can add a nice cushion to the Emotional Bank Account. We'd be fools to blow them off.

The Friendship Debate

> "You can be friends and parents at the same time. Like, if my parents are being cool about things in general, I'll tell them other stuff that's going on. I like my parents and everything, but if they're being assholes, I freeze them out. Anyway, cool parents can be both."
>
> —Katie, 15

So often in parenting our teenagers, I think we are missing the boat. It seems to me there are two prevailing modes of thought out there these days on how to approach the parenting and discipline of adolescents correctly. In one mode, you want to be your kid's best buddy, and all discipline goes out the window. In the other, you're an authoritarian parent, all discipline and no fun. Yes, the conventional wisdom of the day dictates that we are charged with being parents, not friends, to our children. There is a dichotomy here, a divide between parenthood and companionship with one's teenager.

Too many parents, it is believed, are trying too hard to be buddies with their kids. The result, it is feared, is a child who is spoiled, who does not have a reasonable sense of the realities of life, and who pays an enormous price for this buddyhood later in their lives. I suppose this is true to some extent. Perhaps this is partly a matter of semantics as well. I think by referring to "friendship" in this context we really mean to cite some of those parenting methods that never work, including micromanaging and coddling. Of course, I agree that serving purely as a "friend" to your child, sans the requisite boundaries and structure provided by an available parent, is not effective parenting.

That stated, though, it is important to note that we are not our teenager's *enemy* either, nor do we want to be. This black-or-white deal leaves us with precious little middle ground. Yet I believe that almost all of parenting takes place somewhere in that middle ground. The concept of availability will provide you with a guide to successfully navigating this gray area, the middle ground. After all, we want to be *friend-ly* with our teen, don't we? Why would a teenager in his right mind listen to, or heed the words of, someone he considered an adversary or a jerk? And furthermore, we want to enjoy our teens, don't we? I don't want to see you over-correct for this friendship principle to the extent that your rela-tionship with your teenager becomes adversarial. To my thinking, that defeats the whole reason for parenting.

SHIFTING THE ENERGY

Here's an easy one.

If you want to communicate better with your teenager, talk with him about things that interest him. Recently I coached a young man, David, who began the session by telling me he had had an awful week. He went on to describe a litany of events that were going wrong in his life: his grades were terrible; he was arguing with his parents daily about drinking, homework, and curfew; he felt repellent to girls, and on and on. David seemed quite depressed, and his energy was undeniably low. I listened politely to what he had to say, nodding appropriately as we thera-pists tend to do, and acknowledging that this must indeed be a difficult time for him. Honestly, however, after a few complaints, I felt my attention waning and my energy depleting as well, and I was wondering how I would make something useful out of such an overall negative hour.

After David completed his oration of problems and his posture had deteriorated from upright to gently slouching to the left of the couch, I said, hoping to inject a bit of humor into the session to lighten things up, "Well, this has been fun." Sensing my sarcasm, he agreed that it had *not* in fact been fun, and I followed up with, "So what's *working*, man?"

What followed blew me away. David sat up on the couch, leaned forward, and started telling me about a show he had watched the previous evening on The History Channel. He talked about how little we knew about sea life deep on the ocean floor, describing in great detail the nature of the biology required for survival there. He went so far as to pantomime the look of some of these odd creatures so that I could better understand their oddities. And just like that, we found passion. But don't be fooled: the first part of the conversation was important. David felt heard and validated. In the latter part, though, he found himself again: his joy, his passion, and his energy. If I hear 10 years from now that David has become a renowned marine biologist, I will not be a bit surprised. Amazing what a little shift in energy can do.

Granted, the conversation did not necessarily go where I wanted it to go. Hell, I did not even *know* where I wanted it to go—just somewhere different from where it had been. Yet in the end, we found David's energy, passion, and enthusiasm. All it took was a recognition of my own depleted energy and a subsequent shift in the focus of the conversation. David left the session with a spring in his step, and I would argue he felt good about the session—listened to and respected. He was eager for our next meeting and suggested I check out the show on THC as he was leaving. In fifty minutes, David moved from depressive, low-energy, negative thinking to high-energy excitement and enthusiasm. I had trouble getting him to end the session! And really, aren't we all like that? Find our passion, and off we go. I know that describes me pretty well.

What a remarkable, simple little lesson. Engage teenagers in something they're interested in, and they tend to be willing to talk about it. If you're a busy parent, and who among us is not, you really need to take a moment, take a deep breath, or two, or three, and really protect time for this type of conversation. But a note of caution. If you're in hurry-up mode, your teenager will sense it, and the opportunity for communication will be lost. So turn off the cell phone, take a deep breath, and get into it. Talk about your kid's interests. Ask him questions. Debate with him. Have fun, and enjoy your time together!

I have heard from far too many teenagers that they feel their parents don't truly care about them, and they will accurately cite Mom's inattentiveness or Dad's focus on work over them as a priority. A couple of weeks ago, in a family session, I caught a dad stealthily checking his e-mail on his Blackberry while his daughter was talking. At the time, this was kind of funny, I suppose— certainly another clear illustration of how very addictive these devices can be. But think about the message this teenager comes away with: *Even for this one short hour, when we are here to focus on me, and my relationship with them, my dad cannot put that thing down.* It was painful, really, because in that moment the father validated many of the assertions his daughter had made about him in sessions. Thankfully, this family was open enough to make this inattentiveness the focus of the conversation for a while, leaving open the possibility of hope for change.

RE-CONNECTING

> "Parents should be their kids' allies, not
> their enemies, right? I mean, why not? Are
> we supposed to just hate each other for the
> rest of our lives? What's the point of that?
> Don't be hatin,' man!"
>
> —JACK, 16

As you read this section, I encourage you, despite any current circumstances or conflicts, to recall the strong connection you once felt with your child. Even if it's been years.

A few years back, I watched an interview with Paul Simon, reflecting on his professional life. Despite his obvious genius as a songwriter and singer and all the worldwide acclaim, he admitted that he still does not see himself as successful. He cited his father's lack of approval and support as the reason for his discontent—specifically, his father never told him he was proud of him—which kept him from feeling and enjoying his own success. It was a sad and striking moment to witness. We can have the entire world telling us time and time again how wonderful we are, but without the unconditional love and approval of our parents, it all quickly becomes meaningless. When I make decisions about my career, I still consider what my father would think, and he died more than a decade ago. If we still feel this way about our parents all these years out of childhood, how can we really expect our children to feel any differently about us today?

Know this. Teenagers simply want a voice, to be heard. You know, just like everyone else. When you shut them out or cut them down when they begin to express that voice, they will withdraw—from you, from themselves, perhaps even from that voice. That's when you might be the recipient of a big, shocking "Fuck you!" But do not believe for a moment that your child doesn't want your approval, to feel connected to you—despite what he may say and do, your teenager wants nothing more than that connection. True, he wants and needs to feel connected to his friends as well, but do not underestimate the importance to him of his connection with you.

And be prepared to experience a shift. As you begin to foster an improved connection with your teen, you will see her open up to you more, lighten up more, find more motivation and inspiration. The result may not look exactly as you envision. I encourage you to trust that whatever the result, it is exactly as it is supposed to be, and as long as you are available, you are doing the best, most inspired job you can as a parent.

I recently worked with a father and his teenage son, James, in a session. They came in, sat on opposite ends of my couch, and began to bicker, beginning with a barrage of questions from Dad:

> *"Did you take the car out last night without asking? What time did you get home? Tell the doctor. What are you getting in Math, right now? Is your homework done today? Why do you treat me with such disrespect?"*

Predictably, James quickly began to freeze Dad out. To Dad's credit, he sensed this and changed his tack, raising his eyebrows and adopting a more empathic-sounding tone:

> *"You know I love you. I just want you to learn some skills so that you can do better! You know, study and organization skills. Without these things, you know, James, the real world can be a very difficult place. You*

*have got to find what motivates you. And the video
games, we've got to make it so you play those less too.
Are you hearing me here? James?"*

Ah, the futility of the lecture. I could so easily see that James had
heard it all before, countless times. Couldn't his father see this
as well? How could he miss the fact that James just glazes over
and stares off into a corner of the room, like clockwork, once any
lecture begins? In any event, no matter what therapeutic tactic I
tried, I could identify no common ground. Father and son simply
could not seem to connect in this session—they never even looked
in each other's direction. It was apparent that this was the tenor of
their conversation all the time. Now, I often check in with my own
emotions during sessions as a guide for my next words or intervention, and in this session I consistently felt sad and empty. It was
truly a pathetic scene and unfortunately one I had witnessed in
one way or another more times than I can count. Heartbreaking.

Not until I asked the two of them what they used to have in
common was there any movement:

*"I don't know if you'll remember this, but when you
were little, I used to take you to Bulls games when I
could get tickets. You were a funny kid, because on
one of the best teams ever, with Jordan and Pippen
both on the floor, your favorite guy was Paxson,
remember? Paxson over Jordan, for God's sake! Do
you remember that?"*

James smiled and nodded, almost imperceptibly. The spark of a
distant, nearly lost connection began to reignite, proving, to me,
that hope for a connection is never lost. We leave the mini-crises

of the here and now to talk hoops from a bygone era, a much more important conversation. The spark is gently stoked. And father and son leave remembering that underneath all the superficial day-to-day bullshit, they actually love each other.

We need more moments like this with our teens, little reminders of our connections. Too often, I have seen parents forfeit their relationship to the frustrations of the moment, as James's father was at risk of doing right before my eyes. Like him, dig into the past for that connection and spark if it works. Or find something in the present where you can, for a moment or two, touch base, see eye to eye, or even engage in a good-natured debate. The connection, after all, is the core of your relationship. It is the foundation of resilience that makes your relationship less vulnerable to the storms of adolescence. Without this foundation, this core, your relationship and all the love and wisdom within it will simply be thrown asunder. Be available to nurture the core, and the strength of your connection will carry you both through.

"Get My Parents off My Back"

In individual sessions, I would have to admit that the most common therapeutic goal I hear from teenagers is "Help me get my parents off my back." Okay, perhaps it is not particularly therapeutic. There may be times when you hear this from your teen as well. "I just want you to leave me alone!" or "I need my space, man!" Many parents, of course, take immediate offense to this sentiment. But I caution you to remember that these feelings are developmentally appropriate, feelings you likely felt during your teen years.

Now, I find these statements mean different things to different kids. Find out what it means to your teen, because it is likely more than just the rant of a hormonal adolescent. More often than not, it is also *true*. In my therapy and coaching work, therefore, I sometimes choose to align with this goal instead of trying to talk a teen out of it: "Okay, *how* are we going to get your parents off your back? What control do you have here? What can you do to give them some peace of mind so they let up on you?"

Now, these are questions you parents can ask of your teens as well. Again, instead of taking offense, I would encourage you to place your ego aside in favor of curiosity. This particular intervention can lend a sometimes fun, playful tone to what would otherwise surely be dead-serious conflict. These kinds of questions will not only lighten the emotional load, but will put you in a problem-solving mode with your teen:

"*So you feel I'm on your back. I get that. What do you think we can do to change it?*"

"*Well, I have to start doing at least some of my homework, I guess, or you'll never get off my back.*"

"*Good point, Jimmy. That would probably be a good start.*"

"*And maybe I can do some stuff around here without being asked, like, fifteen times. Like take out the garbage or something.*"

"*Yes. That would get me off your back pretty quickly.*"

And now you're communicating.

PROTECT TIME

> "There are days when I want to do things with my dad, but he can't. I'm not mad when he can't do these things, because I know he's not doing it to hurt me."
>
> —JEFF, 12

STEP AWAY FROM THE iPHONE!

A critical component of availability involves clearing out the clutter in our lives that we allow to routinely, often insidiously keep us from sincerely attending to our children—clutter that keeps us from being fully present in the relationship. On a recent evening, my wife, Julie, pointed out that though our family was spending time in the same room together, we were all staring into different screens. In America today, I'll bet there are many households in which this separate screen time counts as quality time, but it is not. Julie rightly noted that this was depressing to her, and we started spending our time together differently, even if it sometimes meant all of us staring at the *same* screen.

Sometimes availability is a deep psychic concept, the removal of your emotional blocks as a parent, facilitating your ability to fully engage with your teen. Other times, on the other hand, it's far less complex and more *obvious*.

As parents, we find sly excuses to slip away from our most important relationships, don't we? A friend of mine told me her husband spent a recent Sunday watching football, then baseball (since when can we watch both of these on the same day, anyway?), effectively ignoring his kids all day and night. But of course, it was the playoffs, so we make an exception. Or the season finale of *American Idol*, so we make an exception. And, with enough exceptions, with hundreds of channels of TV and a DVR on over-drive, we allow our time to be slowly chipped away. This can be a slippery slope—only when we step back and take an honest look does it become obvious. Beware aware of allowing too many exceptions. When in doubt, be available for your kids. You never get this moment back. It's precious.

Last Father's Day, my family and I set out to escape the 90-plus-degree heat at our neighborhood swimming pool. Throughout the pool and the surrounding grounds, families were gathered talking, laughing, playing, and eating. My son and I were in the pool entertaining ourselves devising a variety of games involving the throwing of balls and splashing. A man from the neighborhood arrived with his son, and as they applied sunscreen and picked out a ball themselves, it looked like they were planning to do the same. They both hopped in the water, and this dad threw a ball around with his son for a grand total of three minutes. I saw a hint of dejection on the boy's face as he pleaded with his father to continue the game. The boy continued playing alone, save for a few moments playing with my son and me. I could not help but feel that this was a familiar scene for this young man.

Meanwhile, I'll admit curiosity got the best of me. I kept an eye on this father, who was checking his Blackberry, for God only knows what, before he was even dried off. He stared at it, pressed some buttons, and put it down on the table next to his chaise. Not thirty seconds later, he was looking at it again. He went on like this, staring at the tiny screen and pressing buttons, for at least a half an hour. Meanwhile, his son was just feet away playing in the water, alone.

I couldn't help but wonder what could be so important that this guy was willing to give up this precious time with his child. On

Father's Day, no less! What a rip-off, for both of them! The scene only became grimmer as the boy got out of the water to stand by his father's side. Dad appeared too engrossed in the tiny screen to even notice his son vying for his attention. The kid didn't stand a chance. The draw of e-mail was just too powerful!

As another example, I was recently discussing this concept with a good friend, father of three, who travels quite a bit for work. As we talked, he was taken aback to realize that when he passes through the front door on returning home, the first thing that gets his attention is the mail. This man, by the way, is an attentive, loving father. He lamented the message this gave his family and decided to change in an instant. From now on, the mail will wait. Just stop and think for a moment about the subtle messages you might be sending to your kids.

The solution here is almost too obvious, too simple. When you're with your child, turn off the Blackberry. Don't answer the iPhone. The mail can wait. Make eye contact with your child, not the little screen. Let your child know that spending time with him, right now, is the most important thing. Not because you want it to *appear* that way, but because it truly *is* that way.

I could not believe, on Father's Day of all days, that the dad in the story above did not *get it*. And we all know that he is not alone. A week later, I saw another father do the same during a song in the middle of his child's recital. We've all seen many parents talking on cell phones nearly nonstop when with their children. Is this really spending time together, or just passing time *near* each other? Sadly, you can see the future of the relationship as clear as writing on a wall, can't you? If you were ritually blown off, time and again, how long before you'd say, "Screw you. I'm out!" I can tell you with certainty that by the time they are teenagers, some children have already decided.

So stop what you are doing when you talk with her. Look her in the eye. Treat her the way you would demand that someone else treat her!

I know, these are busy times. We have crowded, hectic schedules to keep, work to do, households to run, games and plays to attend, family events to plan. Yet I encourage you to stop and think for a moment right now, as you read this page, about your values. What is important to you? Who in your life is important to you? Do you live in accordance with those values, prioritize your use of time in line with those values? I know that your relationship with your teenager is important to you, or you would not be reading this book right now. Recognize the importance of your teenager in your life and the relationship you have with her. Through your actions, make her the priority that you know she is to you.

Take the time today just to check in with your child, without need or expectation. I guarantee you will not regret doing so.

I should add a final incentive. Over the past few years, many of my clients have been teenagers, boys mostly, referred by their parents for video game addiction. These guys play *Call of Duty*, *Halo 3*, or *World of Warcraft* for hours on end, much to the dismay of their parents. In some cases I believe this can be a serious issue. Other parents have complained that their teen rarely goes a waking or sleeping moment without their earbuds firmly in place. And let's not forget texting, the bane of many a parent's existence. But I wonder whether we parents model this behavior for our teens through our own obsession with electronics, from iPhones and iPads to Blackberrys to flat screen TVs to laptop computers. Yes, folks, in many cases I think we are part of the problem. We need to practice what we preach when we have teenagers. They're smart, and they'll call you on your hypocrisy, leaving you a very thin case to argue.

U CN TXT UR KID, K?

Now, allow me a moment to be contradictory. I am not in fact against all electronic communication with your teenager. I have worked with a number of families who keep in touch frequently via cell phone, and many parents are comforted by the fact that their teenager is only a call away. Further, some families have found texting to be a useful, novel, entertaining way to communicate some of the time. I think texting is a relatively poor substitute for more direct, personal communication, but it certainly beats no communication at all.

There is also a certain reality we as parents need to face here. Texting is among the preferred modes of communication among teenagers. The occasional note, reminder, or little joke keeps you in some contact. I worked recently with a father who had a highly conflicted relationship with his 16-year-old daughter. Every time the two of them were in the same room, an argument would ensue. I suggested the father text his daughter once or twice a day, something nice, benign, not negative or judgmental. He agreed, and their in-person communication began to improve rather quickly. By the way, they continue to send text messages to each other every day. Occasionally, he told me recently, he'll send an "I love you." Once, he got one back. He said that made all the squinting, misspelling, and punching in those little letters more than worth it.

So sometimes the power of the handheld device can be used for good.

EYES UP

I worked with a man who was struggling with absent-mindedness. He claimed he was nearly constantly forgetful, always preoccupied with some project at home or an issue at work. He agreed that he was almost never available in the present moment, for himself or for anyone else. As a result, he would frequently lose things: keys, important papers, even his wedding ring. (This, you might guess, really caused him problems!) He was often late for appointments, including our sessions together.

We struggled to identify a mantra or affirmation that might help him remain more available moment to moment, but we found this task quite frustrating. Nothing we came up with seemed to click for him.

Then, one week, he arrived for his session early, eager to share a revelatory "aha" moment he had recently experienced. He realized that the vast majority of the time his eyes were focused down. He was either staring at a screen or his phone or, when walking, at the ground. Because his gaze was down, he claimed he missed just about everything. And looking down had become so ingrained a habit, he found he was wholly unaware of it at any given moment. His new mantra fell out of this revelation with ease: "Eyes up."

Eyes up.

This changed everything for him. He was no longer forgetful, but focused. He felt more plugged in—to his work, to his relationships, to every facet of his life. This man was a new father. I can imagine that his newborn daughter will benefit enormously from her father's mantra.

I encourage you to try the "Eyes up" mantra for a day. Check in and note the changes it makes in your availability in all areas of your life, but especially in your parenting.

CALM, CLEAR CONSEQUENCES

"My parents give me way too much leeway, you know? Don't be naïve. It makes me think you don't care. Ask me what's going on. And read between the lines. We need, like, guidance."

—PEYTON, 17

DISCIPLINARY ACTION

You may think that if only your teen would adjust her behavior and respond to discipline, by God, all the issues between you would simply diminish. Perhaps you find yourself frustrated with your teen's lack of discipline, unwillingness to follow rules, or propensity for pushing limits on even the simplest of chores or requests. She may, for example, agree to empty the dishwasher, take out the garbage, get started on homework, or clean her room—but you want it done *now*, and she says she'll get to it when she finishes texting her BFF du jour.

You may also think that I want you to go "soft" on "crimes"

such as these. "Well, now, wait right there just a minute, Duffy. Are you telling me that I do not have the right to guide, discipline, or, hell, to *parent* my kid? Where's the receipt for this book? I'm gonna pick up something hard-core and practical, maybe Dr. Phil. Screw this available parenting crap. I need an iron fist here, dammit!"

Okay. I do not mean to imply that you are not entitled, as parents, to *parent*—quite the contrary. Appropriate discipline provides the boundaries and structure our teenagers need, a template for a successful future—all of that. I would argue, though, that without clear, loving communication, you render yourself powerless in your relationship.

Think about it: "Geez, Dad, you haven't talked to me about anything in weeks except what a screwup I am, and now you want to lay into me about my lousy midterm grades. Tell you what, I was going to go out with some pals, but let me cancel my plans real quick, and we can spend some quality time on my disciplinary issues. Why don't we use the living room, where it's comfortable?"

Yeah, that happens.

Oh, and in case you're considering it, the old "Wait till your father gets home" won't work either. I've asked. Scare tactics are effectively, well, *ineffective* in disciplining today's teenager. They'll only serve to widen the gulf between you. Yes, I'm sure.

So, let's discuss what works. First, it is important to remember that discipline is, in effect, structure. Teenagers actually respond well to structure—in fact, they need it. But as they strive for independence, you will sense the conflict between your teen's willingness to conform to structure and his need to pursue his individuality. You will have to choose your disciplinary battles wisely, and the fewer rules, the better: the more rules you impose, the more rule-breaking you foster. This is where you risk micromanaging your teen, not allowing him a wide enough berth to get into some tight spots, problem-solve, and get himself out of them. Again, you want to allow him room to establish his sense of competence, and too tight a rein will prevent him from doing so. Choose your disciplinary battles carefully.

Now, in all interactions, your *intention* as a parent is critical, but never as critical as it is with regard to discipline. If you intend to teach and foster competence and a sense of responsibility through your discipline, I believe firmly that with this clarity you will achieve that result over time. On the other hand, if your intention is to punish your teen through anger, rage, and disappointment, your teen will learn only that you are angry and punishing. Their character will not develop in a way that is adaptive for them, and you will find yourself repeating this technique ad nauseam, with consistently unsatisfying results.

Again, to be clear, available parenting does not disempower you in the disciplining of your teenager. Quite the contrary, all of your disciplinary power comes from availability. If your discipline comes from a calm, centered, loving place, it will be far more effective than discipline that simply conveys anger and frustration. In the latter scenario, you are simply modeling the behavior you do not want to see in your teenager, unwittingly supporting the likelihood that they will respond in kind. This is neither productive nor a lot of fun.

Furthermore, calm, loving, available discipline does not require that you go easy on your teen. Instead, in a calm conversation uncluttered by any immediate crisis, you establish a clear set of rules and guidelines for behavior in your home and in your presence. I encourage you to include your teen in the construction of the contract. This way, they feel more a part of the process and are therefore far more willing to buy into the tenets of the agreement. Written or not, the contract between you and your teen should always be abundantly clear, leaving little or no room for discussion once a rule or guideline is violated. Your teen will feel she has more agency over what takes place because *she* makes the decisions—she can choose whether or not to follow a rule. If she chooses not to do so, the consequences are clear and require a minimum of discussion. More on behavioral contracts in a moment.

Now, remember, we want discipline to represent some small fraction of your interaction with your teen, not the lion's share!

Before we move on, I need to share an important note on the basics of discipline. If your teen has done something that does not meet your approval, I suggest you sit down calmly and discuss the issue with them. "I really disagree with the choice you made last night, going to that party and lying to us about it." Mete out consequences as you see fit. You are the parent. You get decision-making power in these circumstances. Be careful, however, to separate the behavior from the child. It's the difference between saying "That was a foolish decision, and I expect you to make smarter choices in the future," and "You idiot! I can't believe you would do something so stupid!" Too many teenagers label themselves screwups based on their parents' perceptions of a few poor decisions. Talk about the decision, but let your teen know you sincerely believe in him and his ability to make a good decision, to do better next time. Every issue, every screwup, is an opportunity for you to talk and connect. If you make the screwup the endgame of a struggle about his *character*, both opportunity and self-esteem are lost.

PUNISHMENT, REWARDS, AND CONSEQUENCES

Let's keep this simple. You can choose to punish your teen for certain infractions. You know how to do it. As a parent, I think punishing is your right. But I wouldn't. I certainly wouldn't do so very often.

Rather, I encourage you to focus far more often on your teen's positive behavior. I find it much more useful when parents "catch" their teens in behaviors they support and reward those behaviors. My experience tells me that if you choose to focus on what you consider negative behaviors, your teenager is more likely to engage in negative behaviors. Conversely, of course, if you choose to focus on the positive in your communication, you tend to see more of the positive. The law of attraction seems to apply particularly well here.

Punishments also tend to foster arguments and strife on an ongoing basis. But worst of all, I find that the administration of punishment tends to cut off communication. I prefer a method of identifying consequences for certain *nonnegotiable behaviors*, as outlined below, where teens are deeply involved in the process. Most of all, as I repeat time and time again, each screwup or rule violation presents us with an opportunity if we are open and available. I encourage you to take a deep breath when you are inclined to mete out a severe punishment out of anger and think about where the opportunity lies in the situation. Let's face it, we already know that if you have a lecture in mind, your teenager can likely recite it for you. This is part of why lecturing never works. Squelch communication in any way, and you mute your voice in your teen's head, a voice he carries within him as a guide in decision making.

So, punish if you must. But know the risks if you choose to do so, and make sure you are not punishing out of blind anger or rage. The available parent is much more likely to forgo punishment in favor of clear consequences, reinforcement of positive behaviors, and open communication.

THE BEHAVIORAL CONTRACT

I recently led a focus group for parents, both to get a grasp of their concerns and to collect any ideas they might have that would prove useful for other parents. One couple offered a gem of a technique they had been using with their teens for years, which I promptly decided to steal and use in this book.

Once a year, around the beginning of the school year, these parents draft a comprehensive, written behavioral contract, complete with consequences for contract violations. (Note that we are not using the term *punishment* here.) Common transgressions are noted in the contract, including but not limited to such behaviors as violating curfew, ignoring chores, drinking alcohol, and poor grades. All terms are determined through negotiation and delineated in the contract. I would encourage you to list no more than six or seven transgressions. Choose your battles. If it really does not matter whether the bed is made, just shut the bedroom door and leave it out of the contract.

These parents also decided it was important that their children play a role in the formation of the contract. They knew that their teenagers would be far more likely to buy into and abide by a contract they played a role in creating. They made the creation of the contract kind of fun, with legal jargon and signatures and back-and-forth negotiations.

Further, to control the threat of emotional outbreaks during negotiations, these parents decided to draft the contract over dinner, in a restaurant, out in public. No yelling, screaming, or tantrums. No humiliating scene whatsoever. Brilliant. Needless to say, these parents report great success with their contracts. They minimize conflict and negative communication, foster trust and competence, and free up their time with their teenagers for more enjoyable activities. *And* they only need to renew the contract once a year. Is that a great idea, or what? Since learning of this technique, I have suggested it to many of my client families with teenagers. A number of families have implemented these contracts, and I have heard only positive feedback. An outstanding available parenting tool!

Now, I have one additional note to offer regarding this idea. I was out to dinner with friends recently, and I brought up the subject of these parent-teen contracts. In this discussion, a friend of mine clearly indicated his disapproval of such an arrangement, asserting, "Parenting is about judgment, and if you have a contract, your child is not learning to exercise judgment. This contracting stuff is 'helicopter parenting.'" Interesting point. He suggested that a contract might not be useful in all situations but might be a good idea in some.

Because I respect his opinion, I gave his suggestion some consideration and bounced the idea off other parents. Many of them said they planned to implement something like it in their family shortly. After a number of discussions, it became clear that such a contract would best be applied to behaviors considered nonnegotiable: either involving health or safety or behaviors that are especially important to the parents, such as respect for adults and curfew. You cannot, and would not want to, draft a contract that covered all potential behavior.

I have found that a contract *can* allow for judgment to develop. Effectively, through contracting with him, you are letting your teen know that he has choices. He uses his judgment to make decisions based on what he knows about your feelings and based on the contract. Should he choose a behavior included in the contract, the consequence is clearly delineated in the contract—no discussion, debate, or argument is required. Of course, that leaves open the myriad possible behaviors that are not a part of the contract. With these, your child needs to exercise his judgment fully, with you there for guidance and consultation.

Sᴀᴍᴘʟᴇ Bᴇʜᴀᴠɪᴏʀᴀʟ Cᴏɴᴛʀᴀᴄᴛ

The following is a behavioral contract between _____ and his parents, _____ and _____. This contract has been entered into willingly, openly, and without undue force or coercion. The purpose of this agreement is to best ensure _____'s health and safety, to provide clarity of consequences for other nonnegotiable behaviors, to avoid any miscommunication, and to free up our time together for other stuff. This document is in no way to be interpreted as a lack of faith or trust in _____.

That stated, should _____ choose to engage in any of the following behaviors, we all agree that the consequence(s) delineated is(are) reasonable given the nature of the contract infraction. As such, no discussion is required following any infraction other than reference to this document.

Following is a list of behaviors and their agreed-upon consequences:

1. Curfew of _____, with a stipulation that _____ will be allowed home earlier should he so choose.
CONSEQUENCES: _____

2. No alcohol.
CONSEQUENCES: _____

3. All homework completed nightly.
CONSEQUENCES: _____

4. _____
CONSEQUENCES: _____

This contract shall be valid for one year from the date of signing.

TEEN	MOM	DAD

WHEN TO SAY NO: FOLLOWING YOUR INTUITION

"My parents, they do a lot for me. At least
some of the time, they're the bosses."
—SUSAN, 14

I talked to a mom recently whose 16-year-old daughter, Sarah, asked to go to her first concert. This mom wanted her daughter to enjoy this experience, but she had certain conditions and was consulting with me about whether such conditions were reasonable. She wanted to know where the concert venue was, who would be attending, and what time it started. She wanted an assurance that her daughter would not drink alcohol that evening. Finally, despite the fact that her daughter and all her concertgoing friends had driver's licenses, this mom wanted a parent to drive.

Predictably, Sarah was livid: "How humiliating! We can all drive and you won't let us! I knew you would make this too hard! I knew you would ruin this for me! You don't trust me at all!"

Well, right, maybe her mom doesn't trust her. Teens are entitled to your unconditional love. Trust and respect have to be *earned*. And health and safety are nonnegotiables. So Mom chose not to relent this time. In fact, let's empower you as parents right here and now. When it comes to issues of health and safety with your teen, you *always* get the call. I encourage you to listen to your gut, your intuition. So how, you might ask, does one make a close call, one where it isn't clear whether health and safety are really at issue?

If you feel *not quite right* about a given situation or circumstance, you can and should say no, or change the circumstance, as this mom chose to do. And I encourage you to be conservative here. If you feel uneasy about a situation, chances are there is good reason. Follow your intuition. This mother had intuitive feelings and instincts that drove her decision making. She did not want to deprive her daughter of the experience of attending her first big concert, but she was not about to compromise Sarah's safety in the process.

Once you have decided on your approach, I encourage you not to overexplain or discuss the matter much further. Too many words serve to weaken your stance and possibly highlight any doubts you harbor about your position. You are a parent. It is part of your job to make such judgment calls. And do not expect your teenager to be happy, understanding, or grateful. Under normal circumstances, they'll be pissed off. That's just fine.

"I'm concerned about your safety" will suffice. You may very well receive smart retorts: "Kathy's mom will let her go." Your reply: "OK. That's Kathy's mom." Nothing more need be said. Your house, your kid, your rules. Nonnegotiable. Period.

SEE THE LIGHT

> "When you change the way you look at things, the things you look at change."
> —DR. WAYNE DYER

FONDNESS AND ADMIRATION

A few years back, I was doing research for a presentation on intimate relationships. In the process, I read that renowned relationship expert Dr. John Gottman claimed he could predict the viability of a relationship with remarkable accuracy. Specifically, he could tell, often within only minutes of meeting a couple, whether they would still be together in five years. He had collected data from thousands of couples to back up his claims. Pretty amazing.

Well, Dr. Gottman also set out to isolate the variables that fostered longevity in a relationship. As it turns out, two core variables he found to be most important in sustaining a healthy intimate relationship were fondness and admiration. Fondness and admiration. Not whether they fight a lot or resolve their disputes. Not whether they share interests in common. Not even whether they spend a lot of quality time together. Nope, just fondness and admiration. The more time I have spent with couples over the years, both personally and professionally, the more sense Dr. Gottman's findings make to me. Think of couples you know. In those relationships you most admire, I'll bet you'll find that the couple exhibits these two characteristics, fondness and admiration. Together, they can build substantial deposits in the Emotional Bank Account.

Now, keep in mind, Dr. Gottman's research involved intimate couples in committed relationships. Similar research has not yet been conducted on parent-teen relationships, but I would not be at all surprised to find that these same two variables, fondness and admiration, running both ways, are considerable factors in the success and enjoyment of these relationships. I have certainly noted the presence of these factors in the parent-teen relationships that I feel are most successful.

One thing I know for sure: show no fondness or admiration for your child, and she'll have none for you. Unfortunately, I've come across this phenomenon many times. One in particular comes to mind. A divorcing father, Tony was so focused on his bitterness about the end of his marriage that he was entirely dismissive of the needs of his 13-year-old daughter, Jeannette. She in turn told me she felt increasingly disconnected from her father. I think he felt fondness and admiration for her, but his rage in another area of his life trumped showing this to his daughter. Now she far prefers spending time with her mother and has difficulty finding fondness in her heart for her estranged father. How could Tony expect fondness or admiration from Jeannette when he stopped showing them to her?

I believe, then, that an important part of your job as available parents is to provide an atmosphere that allows for fondness and admiration. In order to do so, you have to be willing to know and accept each other and be open to the other's point of view. You need to show your child your available best, your nonjudgmental, open-minded, accepting best.

There is another finding in Dr. Gottman's work that I believe is relevant here. He also found that couples were more likely to remain together the higher the ratio of positive-to-negative interactions between them. Gottman found a ratio of five positive interactions to every one negative interaction instrumental for relational longevity. Again, I think this finding likely translates well to the parent-teen relationship. As I have indicated elsewhere, I see far too many relationships absolutely dominated by negative interactions between parents and teens, an Emotional Bank Account in the red. In some I could track no positive exchanges whatsoever. None! Could this possibly be the dynamic any parent would want in a relationship with his teenager? Not only does this result in a painful dynamic all around, but it can be quite damaging, in particular for the teen.

So I strongly encourage you to keep Dr. Gottman's ratio in mind. It is not necessary, nor practical, nor likely, that you have 100 percent positive interactions in your relationship. But you need to ensure that there is balance and that the scales are *heavily* tipped in favor of positive interactions. Not only is this better for trust and the flow of communication, it also sets the stage for the two of you to better enjoy your relationship—and you do not want to underestimate the importance of that. Attending to this ratio is advice I frequently offer to parents. Balance here is critical.

Let's examine ways to enhance your relationship with your teen through genuine fondness and admiration.

A Daily Meditation

Your teenager is keenly aware of your energy. Every day, protect a few moments to picture the light in him. Regardless of whatever else might be going on in your relationship or the world around you, picture the light in him. Envision him whole, complete, and happy. Be present for him in this way, unconditionally available, every day. You will be amazed at the goodwill your thoughts will attract.

Finding Those Corners Where Strengths Dwell

I talk a lot about how availability is based on the strengths of your teen, not the deficits. But how as parents do we go about identifying strengths? It's not always easy and obvious. It may require you to dig deep for that fondness and admiration.

In your communication with your teen, he may try to shock you. I have worked with a large number of teens who have gained their parents' attention through harsh language, drug references, or open talk about sex. When this happens, there is a good chance that your teen is testing you. Don't take the bait. Don't just get angry and dismiss them when they say, "Well, I'm just going to go get drunk," or have sex, or smoke up, whatever the crime may be.

She may expect you to judge her words or behavior, because other people do. Instead, I encourage you to talk with her, and listen carefully, openly, without judgment; you'll discover invaluable nuggets of information about who she is, how she thinks, and the nature of her strengths.

My client Ross tested his parents in this way. A well-known tagger, he frequently threatened to tag the homes of his parents' friends with his graffiti. He told his irate father that he would keep tagging until he was arrested and thrown in "juvie." Ross was very adept at getting a rise out of his parents, and they shared with me that he scared them to death. Conveniently, I was able to witness this family dynamic at work. In my one-on-one dealings with Ross, I chose not to buy into his scare tactics. I decided I was not going to judge him; I was just going to listen. So I asked him about tagging, how he goes about it, who he does it with, how he ensures he does not get caught. His story, I must admit, was compelling. Honestly, I found myself living out my outlaw fantasies vicariously through Ross's story.

During one session, Ross pulled a photo album out of his backpack. He was going to show me some of his "work." He told me I should be honored, as no adult had ever before seen his "art." I have to tell you, it blew me away. It was astounding, gorgeous. Ross seemed so pleased that I was impressed, but he was more surprised than anything. He expected a lecture. He expected to be shut out. He told me he put off showing me his work for months because he thought I would have him arrested. Instead, I told him how blown away I was by his remarkable talent and that I could easily understand why he would want his work on display.

Over time, he confided in me that he shared his parents' fears about getting caught, but he didn't want to acknowledge it to them. First, they would just tell him to quit tagging. I eventually encouraged Ross to show his work to his parents. Like me, they were so very impressed—they had no idea they had this budding artist in the family. They were open and available enough to see his artistic ability as his greatest strength. We then went about thinking of ways Ross might express himself artistically without getting arrested. He started working on walls sanctioned for graffiti and putting some of his work on canvas. He was commissioned by classmates and colleagues to paint walls in bedrooms and dorms. He is considering going to art school, and eventually he would like to teach art to high school students.

Through this process, Ross became closer with his parents, and through their marked availability, they found a new sense of communion and communication with their son. What an inspiring story!

Now, I don't know whether Ross and his family would have made these connections without the intervention of a relatively objective professional. But I do know that, through openness in communication, a lack of ego and fear, and total availability, you can help your teen identify his strengths as well. As in Ross's case, the greatest strengths are often discovered in the most unlikely places.

SUPPORTING YOUR TEEN'S INTERESTS

> "He's a real nowhere man, sitting in his nowhere land, making all his nowhere plans for nobody."
>
> —LENNON AND MCCARTNEY

In my work, I have heard many parents express dismay because their children showed no passion about anything. I have two thoughts to share regarding this phenomenon. One, it is not reasonable to expect that a teenager is yet well versed in what will become his lifelong passions. This is in fact exceptionally rare. Based on where they are developmentally, I hope that teens will *begin* this process. Remember, though, that adolescence is a time of identity formation. They're figuring themselves out.

If you need them to decide who they are prematurely, they may appear earnestly to do so, but they will likely make any choices early on to please and appease you—to meet *your* ego needs. Their actual development, in the meantime, will likely be arrested. I strongly encourage you to allow your teen to work through this process freely. That said, some kids do find passionate interests and talents early on. I encourage you to support them in these endeavors, cognizant of the possibility that they will evolve and change.

The second thought comes directly from my clinical experience. I worked with a 16-year-old boy a few years back who claimed to have no interests. Further, his actions fully supported his assertion. Max would lie around the house, sometimes watching TV, maybe playing a video game, maybe not. I can remember searching our sessions for his energy, some direction, but months passed and I identified enthusiasm for nothing. Max had no interest in sports, science, girls, money, games, phones, or skateboarding. The list went on and on: Max was interested in nothing. We were truly stuck.

One of our sessions started much like the others, me asking questions, "fishing" for something, anything, to talk about. I asked Max about his musical taste for what seemed like the hundredth time. He said emphatically that he did not like music, and in particular disliked, if memory serves me right, Maroon 5 and Sugar Ray.

> *"These bands they crank out today are soft. They don't play with any heart, and the lyrics are so weak, it's embarrassing."*
> *"Okay, fine, Max, but which bands are better?"*
> *"Nobody's been good for a long time. Zeppelin. They were like, the last good band."*

Pay dirt.

This was the first element of interest this guy had ever shown me. It led to ongoing discussions of classic rock bands, a subscription to *Rolling Stone*, and eventually to the purchase of a Fender Stratocaster and the mastery of bitchin' Zeppelin licks.

And just like that, the boy with no interests, the nowhere man, got busy.

The point is, I think teenagers, all of them, have some interests, some dormant passions. These may take uncovering through a process of acknowledgment and listening. Your teen may be afraid to speak of his interests out loud for fear they'll sound stupid, or he may lack the acumen, ambition, or courage to follow them through. But all teens have interests.

Be curious with your disinterested teenager, and I am confident that as with Max, the outlines of his passions will begin to emerge with time. Be prepared for those shadows to evolve and change shape as they come into focus.

Words with Teens

Our job is an anxiety-provoking endeavor. Patience does not come easy to parents of teens. Instead, we feel a distinct, fresh sense of urgency. We no longer have all the time in the world. Our window of influence is closing, and it feels as if time is speeding up, just as the risks are escalating. We need to act swiftly, make our points with an eye on the clock, time ever more imminent. It feels as if we're packing for college moments after we're starting high school.

The problem is that the more urgent we are, the more inclined we are toward the lecture, the more ineffective our parenting. We're just saying words, and more words, throwing them out, desperate to make a point, hoping they stick.

With highly anxious parents, sometimes my sole immediate advice is to speak only twenty-five percent of the words you're inclined to. The remaining words typically more than suffice.

See, patience is critical, now more than ever. I encourage you to trust the core good nature of your relationship with your teen. Talk less. Listen more.

Talk less. Listen more. You will slow down the pace of your relationship. You will make the impact you need to make.

Breathe. You have all the time you need.

FOSTERING SELF-MASTERY

Availability always works because it is intended to develop a sense of competence in your teen. Self-esteem is derived from this sense of competence. I read recently a suggestion that we abandon the term *self-esteem* in favor of *self-mastery*. The idea is that over the past several years we have drilled our children with ideas of how wonderful they are regardless of whether they have actually *done anything* to merit the accolades. I agree that regardless of the designation—self-esteem or self-mastery—false praise accomplishes nothing genuine, just an inauthentic sense of self. *Master* something in your world, and you will feel good about yourself. Foster this sense of mastery in your children, and they will feel better about themselves. I really don't care what you call it.

I learned a lot about self-esteem, and the lack thereof, some time ago from my 15-year-old client Doug and his family. In family sessions, Doug would consistently make promises to his parents which he did not keep, in fact never had any intention of keeping, and was probably never sure he *could* keep. In retrospect, I wasted countless hours with this family, kidding myself that I was brokering important family deals. Each of these deals was doomed from the outset. From the beginning, Doug did not believe in himself. He was willing, however, to agree to anything that would postpone being chastised and anything that would place him as efficiently as possible in front of his laptop or Xbox playing *Halo 3*. Like his parents, I became frustrated with Doug, never recognizing that he was incapable of truly committing to anything at the time.

Eventually, I realized that Doug was not responding to my behavioral interventions. We began a deeper set of discussions designed to help Doug, his parents, and me better understand his mind-set. It quickly became apparent that Doug held a very low opinion of himself. I turned our attention to Doug's strengths. At first, the list appeared woefully short. He was nice to his friends, and really good at *Halo*, the video game he played for hours a night. Following a hunch, I asked Doug why he was willing to commit so much of his time to this game. First, he said, he really enjoyed the game. But it soon became clear that Doug was very loyal to the other players. We realized that he did not do his schoolwork because *he* was the only beneficiary of that task, but he really came through for others.

Doug eventually got a job at a local grocery store. Due to his hard work and loyalty, he quickly became a highly valued employee. Doug chose to continue this work upon graduation from high school; he is now a department manager and quite proud of his work. It's been years since I worked with Doug and his family, but when I last heard from him, he had returned to school to pursue a degree in management. During breaks, he would work at the store. As far as I know, he has never missed a shift.

Self-esteem comes in strange packages sometimes. This path is not what Doug's parents envisioned for him, but they did realize that it raised his sense of self-worth during the time we worked together, and over time they became very supportive. They were happy that *he* was happy and that he felt good about himself.

I am a big believer in second chances, opportunities to turn things around. If low self-esteem, or self-mastery, or self-worth is a phenomenon that plagues a teenager in your family, I know you have an opportunity to undo the damage, to provide an atmosphere that supports the competence of your teenager so he can go out and successfully take on the world in his own way. Just like Doug.

Now, keep in mind that self-esteem is slippery and elusive for teenagers. Many in my field would argue that our concept of self-esteem does not change much over the course of a lifetime.

Working with teenagers, I beg to disagree, rather strongly. The self-esteem of teens and tweens is an incredibly fickle device, and the meter can shift over the course of hours. A slight from a friend, a slip in a grade, a lecture from you, any and all of these can shift the entire self-concept of a teen immediately.

In his excellent new book *How Children Succeed,* Paul Tough suggests that the ability to self-regulate, to monitor and manage one's own emotions effectively despite circumstance, is perhaps the single most important element contributing to success. Picture a child, or an adult for that matter, who you know well and is self-regulated. Calm under stress and an excellent problem-solver, she is also successful and, on the whole, happy. Her relationships probably flow rather effortlessly, and she likely possesses a strong sense of self-esteem as well. Encouraging self-regulation is also the way to best help our teens create a thread of consistency in their sense of self, a bedrock of resiliency that will make them happier and more successful, now and in the future.

So, you might wonder what we as parents can do to foster this sense of self-regulation in our teens. And the answer is simple and elegant. Support them, let them know you believe in them, and step out of their way. We parents today are too deeply involved in our kids' lives. We dig them out of the holes they create. We check their grades online. We're in constant contact with teachers and coaches. We sometimes try to micromanage even their social lives. Too often, we are doing their job.

But we are doing them no favors in doing so.

Our hair-trigger, anxious parenting styles are robbing our children of the opportunity for self-regulation. How can anyone find a self-concept when their parents are in the driver's seat? Because we are fearful and anxious, we take opportunity away from our kids when they need it most, and when the stakes are reasonable.

Step aside, be available to guide and consult, and the opportunities will present themselves.

And it may not, will not, and should not go perfectly. It's through trial and error and mistakes and corrections that our kids will learn. Trust that you've raised her to be tougher and more resilient than she may appear. She'll surprise you, in a good way.

There is, of course, one other method we can employ as parents to teach our teenagers to self-regulate. We can regulate ourselves. If you have a hair-trigger reaction to adversity, if you externalize blame, if you overtly pity yourself, you are ripe for a self-regulation makeover. As Paul Tough points out in his book, you cannot read a book to self-regulate. It's not about hours spent in the classroom or lecture hall. Self-regulation is, rather, a conscious choice. You need to be aware, present, *available* to the moment in order to self-regulate. And no method for teaching self-regulation could be more effective than modeling.

WHAT ABOUT THE WEIRD KID?

A couple of years ago, the father of a 16-year-old boy requested a session with me. It was intriguing, because he did not tell me much about the nature of his concern beforehand, and unlike most parents, he wanted to attend alone, without his teen in tow. Now, I have conducted hundreds of initial sessions with teens, parents, and families, and presenting problems tend to be pressing issues like depression, anxiety, self-injury, or a severe decline in grades. When I asked this dad what the problem was, he said, quite simply, "Well, the kid's getting weird."

Oh.

So I asked what he meant by "weird." He said his son had blue hair, "not all of it, but just a little," and that he wore "funny pants that hang too low." And that he listened to creepy music. And he didn't want to fish anymore. I asked my usual battery of initial questions, and this dad reported that his son was a nice kid, good student, and a solid new driver. Based on this dad's description, his weird son met the criteria for no mental disorder, not anxiety, depression, or ADHD. As a matter of fact, Dad reported no problems in functioning whatsoever.

I was about to send him on his way when he asked, "Well, wait, Doc. What can we do about the weird thing?"

"Well, nothing, actually."

It turns out that this father was having newfound trouble relating to his son, who was working on individuation and establishing an identity for himself separate and apart from his parents. Part of that was his "weirdness." In the end, Dad was most upset about the growing distance between himself and his teenage son and, in particular, that his son did not want to go on fishing weekends any longer. Dad saw this as indicative of a problem, when in fact it was really more indicative of adolescence. I suggested he approach his son from a place of curiosity rather than judgment. Ask him why he chose to change his hair. And why blue? There must be an interesting answer to that one. And so what if it's weird? That just means it's different from the things that most teens do. Perhaps this dad had instilled in his son a sense of self strong enough that he felt confidence expressing himself in a unique manner. Given that none of the changes he described were dangerous, I suggested that this dad would be best served by embracing, rather than dismissing, his son and the changes in his life. I encouraged him to use the changes as catalysts for discussion and unconditional support.

The bottom line is, sometimes teenagers just choose to be weird. Didn't many of us, in our own way, choose weirdness when we were teenagers? Seems to me there are worse things to be. Weird is interesting and distinctive. For many parents, though, acceptance of the weird does not come easily. There is, of course, a process a parent needs to pass through to get to the point where they accept that their little future banker has chosen a nose ring or black nail polish.

One very peppy, preppy mom came to me a while back, dazed and dismayed, with a deeply insecure daughter, Madeleine, who dressed in a way she described as "thrasher punk." Her mother had other descriptors, including "gross" and "homeless." It took a few sessions with Mom to convince her we had more important things than dress code to worry about with her daughter, so she chose to accept Madeline's dress for what it was. She had to give up the dream, her dream, that she would have a prom queen of a daughter who shared her taste completely, whom she could dress up, take out, and be proud of.

Well, in the end, I was proud of this mom because she did not need Madeleine's mode of dress to be a "phase" either. She just chose to accept it as part of her. Now, one of Madeleine's primary issues was that she felt out of place at home and at school with her peers. In a session, she told her mom and me that she felt as if everyone thought she was weird.

Mom broke the ensuing awkward silence with an enlightened moment of availability: "Well, of course, honey. You *are* weird."

Gulp. I start thinking damage control.

"But weird is good. Look at me. There are a million people around here who dress, look, and talk just like me. It takes *courage* to be and do something different. You have that courage."

In the months that followed, Madeleine would occasionally wear to sessions the WEIRD IS GOOD T-shirt her mother made for her. Somewhere in the process, Mom transformed from ordinary to extraordinary herself. Way to go, Mom!

SHIFTING YOUR ENERGY

I have had parents share with me that although they love their children, they cannot stand them or their behavior an awful lot of the time. I have had a teenager tell me that his mother rejects his hugs when she is upset with him. Did you catch that? This is a *15-year-old boy* who wants to hug his mom and *she* turns away!

Your challenge is this: The next time you feel yourself withholding physically and emotionally from your teen, closing off from him because you are hurt, angry, or disappointed, resist this urge. Turn *toward* him. In that moment, draw in a breath and open your mind, energy, and spirit to him. Feel what changes take place within you. Do you feel differently toward him?

You will find that this simple internal shift toward openness can make an enormous positive impact on the present moment and on your relationship.

BE THE CHANGE

> "This man, my dad, is a man anybody would want for a dad."
>
> —SASHA, 13

INSPIRATION BY EXAMPLE

Perhaps the greatest gift you will ever be able to offer your teenager is the ability to inspire her through who you are as a person—from your value system, to the work you do, to the way you treat others. Your teenager is watching even when you think she is not. I have found that teenagers actually tend to value their parents' judgment and values more than their parents believe they do.

You may think I'm just nuts for suggesting that your teen cares what you think or is in any way attempting to gain your favor. "He does everything in his power to piss me off daily!" I know that's how it may seem, I know. But I repeat, your teen *wants* you to like him, to approve of him, to admire him. As much as the world has changed since you were a child, this has been a constant. Stop and consider for a moment your relationships with your parents. I feel I can safely say that even to this day you typically consider your parents' point of view when making decisions. Would they approve? Will they like it? Will they be angry with me? This is not a bad thing. We want our children to consider what we might think when they are making decisions. This is a part of good decision making.

That is to say, I know you have the clout with your teenager to be an inspiration. He is watching you, and he cares. He probably just forgot to tell you.

The mandate for you, then, is to lead an inspired life yourself. If you find yourself settling in your work, watching TV all night, compromising your integrity, or not taking care of your body, your teens will pick up on these things. Know that they are watching and taking notice. I have had teenagers reveal to me details of their parents' lives that Mom and Dad would be shocked to hear that they noticed, or cared enough to notice. They notice when you're drinking, and when you drink too much. They notice when you drive drunk. They hear it when you tell white lies to a friend on the telephone or when you're gossiping. They notice when you talk about someone behind their back and treat them differently to their face. They notice when you complain about your life, but fail to make changes. They notice every self-deprecating comment you make about your body, your job, your life. They notice when you half-ass it. Believe me, they notice.

So it is important that you find and live your passion, that you take care of yourself and motivate yourself toward growth and self-improvement, for the sake of yourself and your teenager. Remember, you *are* a role model!

A note of caution is indicated here: your child will not be inspired in the same ways as you. He needs to hear his own voice, not yours. As stated earlier, he may find inspiration in some activity or interest that is not at all what you would choose for him. You must note that this is your issue, not his. Support what he wants, follow his desires, and you will discover a happier, more fulfilled teen.

I was recently talking with a high school senior, Gary, who provided me with a great example of parental inspiration. This is one of my favorite stories. He told me that despite working full-time jobs, his parents were always involved in charity work of some kind or another. His mother would volunteer at a women's shelter one night, and his father served on the boards of two different charitable organizations. Joking about this became part of the

THE AVAILABLE PARENT | DR. JOHN DUFFY

family culture. Gary and his siblings would roll their eyes when their parents planned another fund-raiser, joined another board, or attached themselves to some new social cause of the day.

In one session, Gary described a rather difficult decision he had been wrestling with for weeks. He was torn about how he would spend the spring break of his last year in high school. He could fly with a few friends down to Mexico, spending the days tanning and swimming on a beautiful beach and the evenings chasing girls and sneaking a few beers. That one sounds pretty good, Gary. What's the problem? Well, his other option was to caravan down to New Orleans to assist in cleanup and homebuilding in the wake of Hurricane Katrina.

As you might guess, this guy chose the latter. Looking back on the trip, Gary told me about the camaraderie he felt as he worked with new friends tearing down walls. He told me about how his stomach fell when he saw a decaying body of a dog in one of the homes where he was working. He told me about staying up until all hours with his coworkers, laughing a lot, even crying a little. Gary truly felt for the people of New Orleans and seemed eager to get back there to help some more in the summer.

I asked Gary why he made the choice he did. After all, that vacation in Mexico did sound unforgettable—clean and relaxing. He said it just felt like the right thing to do, and he would regret it if he let the opportunity to help pass him by. At the end of this conversation, Gary made a cursory connection between his own charity work and that of his parents. He simply said, "My parents do a lot to help out, too. I guess it's in the blood or something." Clearly, Gary was inspired by the actions of his parents, and he will no doubt go on to make a significant contribution to the world.

I've noticed an unmistakable pattern here: when you choose

to settle for nothing less than the extraordinary in *your* life, your teen will likely do the same in his.

In our busy, hyperscheduled lives, we often forget to give back. Yet many parents I've polled recently have told me they just want their children to be, more than anything else, good people. What better way to foster empathy in our kids, to provide them a context for understanding the world around them, for gaining perspective on their own fears and concerns, than to get directly involved.

ARE YOU A ROLE MODEL?

As has happened so often through the process of writing this book, I recently received a priceless bit of wisdom and insight from a client of mine. Mother to two teenagers, she pointed out the importance of role-modeling through the teen years. She and her husband have made a concerted effort to live the values they want for their teens. Self-proclaimed former couch potatoes, they now work out regularly, volunteer some of their free time, and have become voracious readers. She noted that since they began to have children they let go of some of the activities they used to cherish and enjoy. To their great credit, they decided it would be hypocritical for them to sit around like blobs watching reality TV, while expecting their kids to take on the world. The benefits have proven to be immeasurable. Mom and Dad are more active in the world, sharing their gifts, and their teenagers are inspired to do likewise.

Many of us, I think, believe we are done with modeling when our children are much younger. I have found this to be decidedly untrue. Our teenagers are fully aware of the ways we choose to live our lives. They will see the possibility in dreams for themselves, as they witness you turning your passions into realities every day. Also, and not at all incidentally, working on yourself and your dreams prevents you as a parent from living vicariously through your child, forcing them to fulfill your unmet needs. Free him from your dream so he can find his own.

WHEN *NOT* TO BE AVAILABLE: PARENT AS CONSULTANT

"I want them to take me seriously. They
don't let me make mistakes! The chain's
too tight. They shelter me from making
decisions on my own, and I know that's
not good, right?"

—MASON, 18

We have talked an awful lot about developing a relationship with
your teen, getting to know him, spending quality time with him.
This is all very important for your teen's successful development
into a healthy, happy adult. You may be wondering, though, how
you will find the time to live your own lives while honing this
special new kind of relationship: "How am I supposed to have a
life if I'm constantly available to my teenager?" Good point. Well,
I assure you that you can apply every principle in this book and
still you and your teen will spend the vast majority of your time
apart—as you should. Remember, we are looking to foster the
development of a healthy, *independent* person here.

There will be times—many, many times—in your child's teen
years when you will have to decide whether to get involved, either
in their emotional life or decision-making process. One of the
keys to availability is knowing when to bow out and let your teenager make the call. I recommend this course of action in the vast
majority of situations in which health and safety are not an issue:
Do I study Geometry tonight or go to the basketball game? Should
I break up with her because I saw her talking to that one dude?
Should I go to that party Friday night? Should I get in this car with
these guys? Teens need to struggle through some tough decisions
on their own. If we are always there, always offering advice, we

are taking away from them the opportunity to choose, to learn from a mistake or savor a personal victory, to recognize that they can survive a less-than-ideal situation.

Here again, we need to consider whose needs we are addressing through our actions as parents. Are we acting in the best interests of our adolescent, or are we working to ameliorate our parental anxiety? When you determine that safety is not an issue in a given circumstance, I encourage you to opt for the former. I recommend making yourself available as a parent in those less-than-threatening situations, less as a decision-maker and more as a consultant. You can serve as a sounding board for his thoughts about a given decision, help him to rephrase his position and identify the real-world consequences, and allow him to ultimately make the call.

One of my favorite examples of the utility of parent-as-consultant involves bullying. Since the shootings at Columbine High School more than a decade ago, there has been a media spotlight on bullying among teenage boys. Many in my profession, myself included, developed lectures, presentations, and seminars on how schools can best manage this issue and prevent future school violence. Since that time, with the dramatic increase in social media, a disturbing new kind of bullying among teenage boys *and girls, cyberbullying,* has reared its head, sometimes with devastating consequences.

Like so many issues in the lives of teenagers, there are no absolutely right or wrong answers when it comes to bullying, and I bet you'll be surprised by the wisdom your teenager exhibits when asked about it. In guiding her freshman daughter through this process, one consultant/mom reported that her daughter Cynthia came up with the following options for herself in managing a group of female bullies in the high school hallways:

Walk away.

Glare at them, then walk away.

Ask, "Is there a problem?"

Ask them to sit down and talk about the issue between them.

With her mother's consultation, she decided to try smiling when approached by the bullies and saying, "Hi, guys! How's it going?" and then walking away, smiling. She decided she would react this way regardless of the behavior of the bullies. The mom/consultant in this case reported to me that the technique worked beautifully, and the bullying decreased dramatically. Mom also disclosed that were she the decision-maker, she would have chosen the "Let's sit down and talk" option, which she now thinks would not have worked nearly as well as the option chosen by Cynthia herself.

Now Cynthia has not only stopped the bullies from disrupting her life, but she has an increased sense of confidence that she can handle difficult matters like this. Her mother has remained a consultant, always allowing Cynthia to make the final decision, and that has made all the difference. If there are bullies in this girl's future, I bet she'll have some pretty good ideas about how to silence them. I encourage you to talk with your teen about bullying. If you find in these discussions that your son or daughter is a victim of bullying, put on your consultant hat and guide them through the decision-making process in handling the issue, like Cynthia's mom.

And remember that you are not raising boys and girls. You are raising men and women, husbands and wives, fathers and mothers. You want them to treat others well. You want them to value and care for their families. You want them to be loving spouses and caregivers. You want them to be emotionally intelligent and available parents themselves one day. Foster all of this in your children. Free them to experience the world, make their mistakes, and savor their victories.

Get Blown Away

If you would like to see your teenager in a fresh light, try this little exercise. The next time you encounter a significant dilemma in your own life, be it work-related, relationship-based, or otherwise, run it by your teen. Ask her for her advice. What would she do in the same situation?

Several things may happen. For one, your teenager will feel respected for her point of view. Second, you've got her problem-solving, and it's not even about her behavior, or anything she's done wrong! On top of that, you will have identified another method of connecting with her. Finally, I would not be at all surprised to hear that you found a solution to your dilemma that you might never have thought of.

Be prepared to see your teen at her best. It may be shocking.

I'll bet you're blown away by what you hear.

> "Don't assume I don't care what you think just because I say I don't care what you think."
>
> —JAIME, 15

In my interviews with teenagers, the theme is typically a laundry list of things parents do wrong to turn their kids off, to turn them away. Imagine my surprise when one young man told me he and his parents have "happy" relationships, and that he hopes to be a parent very much like them one day. I finally had the opportunity to ask a teenager what his parents do *right*!

He said they are friendly with him. They just talk to him and really ask him about his life because they want to know him. Unlike his friends' parents, he claims his are trusting and genuine, not accusatory. They make him want to do better and earn their trust, he told me. He does well in school. He works hard in sports and at his job. He's proud of his work, and he likes that his parents are proud of him as well.

In contrast, he told me about a friend's family. He described his friend's parents as authoritarian, angry, mean, and distrustful. His friend, a cigarette smoker, would sneak into the garage at the end of a night out. He would then change into a clean shirt and suck on a mint before heading in the house. He confided that he was "paranoid" that his parents would discover his smoking habit and he would be "grounded for years."

The teen in my office went on to say, "It's so stupid. These parents think they've raised this angel who does whatever they tell him to do. All they've done is scare the shit out of him, so that he does crazy stuff like this. He's no angel. That's just what he *has* to show to them. He's in hiding. They have no idea what the reality is, though. No idea!"

I asked him how he handled the cigarette issue with his own parents. He stated, emphatically, "Oh, I don't smoke. I would never do it. My aunt died of lung cancer, and I could never put my parents through anything like that."

Oh. Well, what about other drugs?

"No way. If I did hard drugs, I'd be violating their trust. It would suck, for all of us. It's not worth it."

My hand to God, these are quotes from an *actual* 17-year-old boy.

So this young guy, who is openly fond of his parents, advises you to be friends with your kids. Let them like you. Don't chase them away with your fear. He went on to indicate that your relationship may *seem* more productive if it's more authoritarian, but you can't really enjoy each other this way. He finished by telling me he'd much rather have the compassion he feels for his parents than disdain. This is what available parenting looks like in action.

You will find that letting go and trusting that you have provided your teen what he needs to navigate the world is among the ultimate rewards of parenthood. Eric Zorn, a columnist for the *Chicago Tribune*, wrote the following about supervised driving for his 16-year-old son:

"Even as you enjoy the experience with a depth you never could have imagined, you always know that the goal is for you to become unnecessary, and that the time for independence will come before either of you are really ready."

Oh, the bittersweet nature of parenting. Yet a critical component of available parenting is recognizing when that time has come, when he is ready to take the wheel and head out into the world. It happens in many little steps and stages over the adolescent years. Available parents are keenly aware of when to step aside.

Now, I do not want to underestimate the sense of loss that accompanies these changes. As parents, it is important that we allow ourselves to experience this loss, balanced with the accompanying joy that our child is moving into a different phase of her life. If we remain stuck in grief that our baby is no longer our baby, we miss the beauty of her maturing and growing, the fruits of our time together. It's not that we no longer play a role, but our role must change. We want to continue to be there, to be available, and see our relationships flourish in increasing shades of maturity, depth, wisdom, and humor.

How to Be "Perfectly" Available

A lot of us are perfectionists. We grab onto a concept, dig in, and try to embody it wholly. As I speak to more parents about availability, I'm always pleased when people get it. I love a nodding audience, because there is not much to this concept we do not already know. We just need to be reminded, and for that reason, I encourage you to keep this book close. Fear, judgment, and ego are slippery, and can ease their way back into your life undetected.

On occasion, though, I talk to a parent who is overly eager, deciding to be *perfectly* available to her children all the time. I always remind them, and I'll remind you here, that part of the elegance of availability lies in its imperfections. I never expect anyone, myself included, to be perfectly available all the time. Given human nature, it's an unreasonable expectation, and there is a rigidity to perfectionist thinking that is antithetical to availability.

We want to make inroads, shift our energy, be more present to moments, and pay better attention. We need to remind ourselves to be available every day, perhaps several times a day. That's okay. That's the right way to be available.

And trust me, this gets easier with time. And availability is a positive feedback loop. The more available we are, the more satisfying our relationship with our teens, the more empowered they feel, and the more connected we feel.

And we are inclined to be more available. You will know, because it will feel better. It will feel right.

FINAL NOTE: MY HOPE FOR YOU

I hope you feel now that your charter as the parent of a teenager is clearer. You now have a blueprint to be fully available to your teen. You know what you can do to foster in him a sense of competence and self-esteem. You know how to strengthen your relationship, such that it is resilient to any storms his adolescence may bring. And best of all, you can now enjoy, with a sense of awe and wonder, your incredible child, your remarkable teenager.

One of my favorite quotes comes from a brilliant psychologist, Virginia Satir. She writes:

Feelings of worth can flourish only in an atmosphere in which individual differences are appreciated, love is shown openly, mistakes are used for learning, communication is open, rules are flexible, responsibility is modeled, and honesty is practiced.

It seems so simple, doesn't it? Applying Dr. Satir's words to our work here, feelings of self-worth and competence in teenagers are born from availability in parents.

My wish for you is a warm, loving, fun, funny relationship with your child throughout his teen years. I hope your challenges together are few but fruitful. I hope you experience the joy that unconditional love and acceptance can bring in even the darkest of times. I hope time spent on discipline and conflict is eclipsed in your home by the sounds of talk and laughter. I hope you take time each day to be grateful for his presence in your life and to see him with wonder.

Embrace the joy. Let go of the fear.

Be the available parent.

ABOUT THE AUTHOR

 Dr. John Duffy is a highly sought-after clinical psychologist, certified life coach, parenting expert, and proud parent. He has been working with teens, tweens, and their families for more than fifteen years. He has provided the critical intervention and support needed to help hundreds of families find their footing.

John is proud to be a regular parenting and relationship expert on the new *Steve Harvey* show and *The Morning Blend* on NBC. His radio credits include NPR, WKRP, the nationally syndicated *Mr. Dad, Bobblehead Dad,* and many more. He has also contributed to a number of print and online media. These include the *Huffington Post, Good Housekeeping, Redbook, Cosmopolitan, Teen Vogue,* AOL, Psych Central, SheKnows, eHow, and Yahoo, to name a few. Video, audio, and article excerpts can be found on his website, www.drjohnduffy.com. He blogs on availability and communicates regularly through his fan page on Facebook and Twitter. Dr. Duffy also speaks nationally on parenting and other relationships.

John lives outside Chicago with his wife Julie and teenage son George.

TO OUR READERS